D0787922

INTUITION

Milton Fisher

INTUITION

How
to Use It
for
Success
and
Happiness

E. P. Dutton   New York

Published in the United States by E. P. Dutton, Inc.,
2 Park Avenue, New York, N.Y. 10016

Library of Congress Cataloging in Publication Data

Fisher, Milton
  Intuition, how to use it for success and happiness.

    1. Intuition (Psychology)   2. Success.   3. Happiness.
I. Title.
BF311.F49   1981   158'.1   81-7790
                                          AACR2

ISBN: 0-525-93209-7

Published simultaneously in Canada by Clarke,
Irwin & Company Limited, Toronto and Vancouver

Designed by Nicola Mazzella

10 9 8 7 6 5 4 3 2 1

First Edition

Contents

Acknowledgments

Everyone I have ever met on my journey through life contributed to this book. I thank them all for the millions of bits and pieces that comprise the mosaic of this work. However, there are those whose help was more specific and generous, and I'm delighted to have this opportunity to acknowledge them.

First, the keepers of accepted knowledge, those with impeccable left-brain credentials, against whose minds I tested my theories: Dr. David Atkinson, scientist, Los Angeles, California; Dr. Donald Payne, psychologist, New York City; Dr. James Fishkin, philosopher, Yale University; Alfred Plaine, retired executive, Pyramid Publishing Company; Dr. Jessica Gross Schairer, clinical psychologist, New York City; Dr. Paul Walton, geologist, Massachusetts Institute of Technology; Dr. Donald Golden, Detroit, Michigan; Herman V. Traub, Doctor of Jurisprudence, New York City.

Second, I'd like to thank those experts in the literary world who encouraged and goaded me to eventually write a book so different from my original plan. Howard Cady, the dean of American editors, William Morrow and Company, and his insightful and charming wife, Marge Cady; Constance Schrader, enthusiastic editor and bestselling author in her own right; Lois Alcosser, creative director and writer; Jane Everhart, writer; Dan Wickenden, Senior Editor, Harcourt Brace Jovanovich, and Anita Diamant, literary agent.

Third, the wonderful people who did the typing, checking, assembling, etc.: Lori Burger, Mildred Ouslander, and Maureen O'Beirne.

Fourth, my fantastic daughter Dr. Shelley May Fisher Fishkin, of Yale University, who squeezed time from her own frenetic activities to do all of the things outlined above and more.

Fifth, the hundreds of students in my Applied Creativity courses over the years whose eager minds, fueled by the passion to find, absorb, and improve, created a living laboratory where many of my ideas were germinated and tested.

This book is dedicated to my friend, wife, and lover Carol Plaine Fisher, who served as the *corpus collosum*, or connecting tissue, with the worlds around me as I grappled with the book. An author in the heat of creation is not the easiest person to live with. Her understanding, intuition, and patience were superb. I have come to realize that the best way to get a great editor is to marry one!

Caveat

This book is a course in how to change your life through the cultivation of your intuitive awareness. It should not be read in one or two sittings. It is meant to be digested and assimilated. The goals it talks about, the insights, the exercises, the ways of knowing are meant to become a part of you. A quarter of a century of teaching others has taught me that change comes in small bites. Read this book one or two chapters at a time. The ideas and suggestions are to be thoroughly chewed, so that you can fully savor, enjoy, and employ what's in them as they become integrated into your way of life.

The apparent simplicity of the ideas and exercises does not vitiate their importance or effectiveness. If you would like to explore more deeply, the Suggested Reading section lists the sources on which this book is based.

Much of my discussion covers the "conscious system" and the "intuitive system." In the interest of brevity and clarity, I often refer to them simply as "conscious" and "intuitive," respectively.

Part I

IN ESSENCE

- Every human being has two systems of awareness, conscious and intuitive.
- During your life your intuitive system amasses a vast mine of nonverbal knowledge.
- This knowledge is expressed through feelings, symbols, dreams, or fantasies.
- The meaning of each feeling, symbol, or dream is unique to you.
- Thus the experience of an intuition can be interpreted only by you.
- Our culture has conditioned you to trust only conscious knowledge and to suppress or to ignore intuitive knowledge.
- This deprives you of vital information you could use to make decisions or solve problems.
- By encouraging your intuitive system to contribute its special knowledge and by being more receptive, you improve your ability to cope with life and enhance its enjoyment.

1

Intuition: What It Is and What It Can Do for You

I've talked with and studied the most successful traders in the securities business to find out how they do it and it comes down to this: They get a feeling and they act on it. All the statistics in the world and all the so-called inside information isn't worth a damn against a gut feeling.

— Charles Srebnik, Wall Street
Investment Specialist

Call it hunch, insight, inspiration, revelation, foreshadowing, foreboding, gut feeling, or inner voice. Today it's sometimes called "vibes." Whatever you call it, there is a little-used but powerful tool at your command that can help you recognize and achieve the success and happiness you want. It is your own untapped, often overlooked, but nevertheless highly effective intuitive system.

Intuition is widely used by successful people. But they treat it like a black-market commodity: It is rarely discussed, acknowledged, or given much credit. Since the Age of Reason, intuition has fallen into such disrepute that most ordinary people are a little ashamed of using it and won't admit to it even to themselves. It is as though they had decided to work with only one hand, when two hands are available.

Almost everyone has had an unforgettable intuitive experience. As a child, I was impressed when my mother would say that her "women's intuition" told her that something was a better course of action — and she invariably was right. My father scoffed, saying, "The bank won't lend you any money on women's intuition, and the trains don't run on women's intuition!" Nevertheless, I noticed that when my mother said, "Sam, my intuition tells me not to trust that man," my father would follow her advice and avoid doing business with him. My intuitive sense has grown from a faint annoying feeling into a powerful guiding force. The ease with which I was eventually able to recognize and act on intuitive messages, and the invaluable aptness of the messages, built confidence in my own intuition. Today I would no more question my intuitive sense than I would question my sight or hearing. Intuitive input has a profound influence on everything I do and on every decision I make.

For the past seventeen years the theories and exercises I've developed for revitalizing intuition have been perfected through teaching a course called "Applied Creativity — Problem Solving Techniques." The course, under the aegis of the Continuing Education Program for Adults in Westport, Connecticut, has changed the lives of hundreds of my students by teaching them how to use their intuitive system for finding creative solutions to the problems they face.

WHAT IT IS

Intuition has saved my life. When I was covering the Olympics in Mexico, it was intuition that made me move for cover when the students were fired on — so I was wounded instead of killed. Intuition is faster and surer than reason.

— Oriana Fallaci

Intuition is knowing something without being aware of how you know it. It is knowledge that seems to come to you from nowhere, a sudden awareness or insight without any logical evidence. The knowledge cannot be traced, but it is real, from the vague shadow of a feeling to a thunderbolt of understanding!

The intuitive system is an awareness network that gathers and processes information that is nonverbal and therefore not part of conscious awareness. When some facet of this "knowledge" breaks into consciousness you have the phenomenon of intuition.

For many people, the "unaccountability," or lack of concrete evidence for this knowing taints intuitive knowledge. They are afraid to rely on it, so they reject it, discredit it, or ignore it.

This is a terrible mistake because the intuitive system is part of man's primordial arsenal for survival. It derives from a time before man had language. Without language, inductive or deductive reasoning is very limited. Primitive man had only his senses and his nonverbal intuitive mind to warn him of danger. This intuitive system remains in all of us as a residual force.

We all have two distinct systems of awareness: conscious and intuitive. Each system records, "thinks," feels, and remembers in its own way. The conscious mind is able to verbalize what it experiences, and this verbalization is a kind of feedback that gives us a sense of security and confidence. The intuitive system is nonverbal. Imagine two cameras running at the same time. Each camera records specific details of the same scene. The *conscious-awareness* camera records the signals received by the five senses — seeing, hearing, smelling, feeling, tasting. These are immediately organized into "logical" sequence and processed by the conscious mind. The *intuitive-awareness* camera picks up another set of signals from the same senses. It processes, organizes, and records them. But it does not develop the film to consciousness. The information is stored for use, for development to consciousness at a later time.

The mind's intuitive awareness system is so efficient that it picks up millions of bits of information that completely elude the conscious or logical mind. It stores this information continually, throughout all the years of your life. As a result, you have amassed a vast storehouse of unconscious knowledge, information that you use whether you realize it or not. Indeed, intuition affects much of what you do and what you think. Your intuitive mind never lies dormant. As a conscientious member of your mental-physical high-command survival team, it is always trying, through symbols, dreams, and feelings, to bring its information to your attention. But alas, it is often ignored, derided, or rejected. This is to your detriment and frustrates your ability to achieve and cope.

Bringing intuitive information to your conscious mind is like a spark jumping the gap between two conductors. In order to tap the rich source of intuitive knowledge you possess, you must learn to bridge that gap between the conscious and intuitive awareness systems.

Is intuition, in fact, a sixth sense? I know of no study that has been able to prove that it is. My research for this book included thousands of interviews over many years with people from every walk of life. The interviews uncovered an almost universal belief that intuition is a form of ESP or extrasensory perception. Extrasensory perception is knowledge gained from a source outside the five senses.

Most ESP experiences fall within one of the following categories:

1. *Telepathy or mind reading* is awareness of another's thoughts without any communication through the sense channels.

2. *Precognition* is awareness of future events or future thoughts of another, often identified as premonition or divination.
3. *Clairvoyance* is awareness of the existence of an object or event in the present or past without use of the senses; sometimes called second sight.
4. *Psychokinesis* is the ability to influence a future event or affect a physical object solely by thought control, i.e., levitation, stopping or starting watches, influencing the fall of dice, and so forth.

Dr. C. E. M. Hansel, chairman of the Department of Psychology at the University of Wales, in his book *E.S.P. and Parapsychology, a Critical Re-evaluation* (Prometheus Books, 1980), examines in great detail the scientific research and evidence used to support the theory of ESP and finds it wanting, i.e., not proved. Nevertheless, that does not mean that there is no such thing as ESP — there very well may be, and perhaps we may still have proof within our lifetime.

But whether ESP exists is not important to the understanding of the intuitive. Intuition does not rely on a sixth sense; it is knowing without being aware of how you know. Our present understanding of how the brain works provides us with a cogent explanation for this phenomenon. There is an overwhelming sea of awareness we all possess that never reaches consciousness. This is subliminal knowledge gleaned by the senses that completely bypasses consciousness. When some aspect of this awareness surfaces into the conscious, it is an intuition.

So when you have an intuitive insight, it is not something coming to you from outer space, but rather information you've gathered and stored through your five senses on a subliminal level. This awareness is not infallible, no more so than your conscious knowledge, but it should be treated with the same respect and attention that you treat information brought directly to your conscious mind by the five senses.

It is obvious, then, that this important data repository can be tapped for guidance. Learning to use it can make some dramatic changes in your life.

Some people seem naturally able to extract and use intuitive information from the world around them. They seem to reach conclusions, solve problems, and sense reality directly, easily, and in a mysterious way that others cannot. We usually conclude that they are more intelligent, more sensitive, and more creative. But very often these "gifts" are just the benefits of intuitive awareness — something we all can develop.

Creative people perform amazing feats because they are able to draw upon their pool of intuitive knowledge. They call this ability "inspiration" or "talent" or their "muse." Actually they have learned to analyze a problem and then add their intuitive knowledge to their conscious knowledge. They seem to come up with solutions to perplexing problems instantly, miraculously, when in fact they have only zipped through the problem-solving steps faster and more productively with the help of their fund of intuitive knowledge.

The ability to solve problems, creative or practical, in every aspect of life, is profoundly influenced by the knowledge you have available. When your pool of nonverbal knowledge is tapped, your problem-solving ability will be enhanced to its greatest potential.

WHY NONVERBAL KNOWLEDGE EXISTS

Is there a scientific basis for the belief that the intuitive mind exists? Recently scientists have speculated on this phenomenon and it has been discussed as part of the "split brain theory."

We have known for years that the right and left sides of our bodies are controlled or dominated by the opposite half of our brain. What we see with the right eye is relayed to the left hemisphere of the brain and what the left eye sees is processed by the right hemisphere. When there is damage to the right side of the brain, there is paralysis of the left side of the body and vice versa.

The two hemispheres of the brain are connected by a nerve tissue called the *corpus callosum*. In the early 1950s, Professors R. W. Sperry and Donald E. Meyers, of California Institute of Technology, conducted experiments and discovered that when the *corpus callosum* was cut, each hemisphere functioned independently, almost as if it were a brain complete in itself. Postulating that we actually have two brains makes it easier to understand how the intuitive system works.

Let us accept, for the moment, that those of our forebears blessed with two brains had a better chance of survival than those with one brain. Over the centuries of evolution the two brains began to specialize. What functions were developed? Research experiments indicate that the left brain today specializes in verbalization, logic, analytical thinking, talking, reading, writing, mathematical calculations, and most linguistic concepts. The right brain specializes in perceptual insight, musical ability, tactile sensation, holistic understanding, and *intuitive understanding*. As a result of this specialization, our thinking and our actions are dominated by our left brain. The right brain is called the "mute" side because it cannot verbalize or articulate. It cannot put into language the information that it has. Since language is needed in the process of logical thinking, the right hemisphere might be called the nonthinking brain. But, we know that it *does* receive, store, and process information in a kind of thinking we do not yet understand.

A series of dramatic experiments by Michael S. Gazzaniza were reported in the *Scientific American* in 1967:

> The experiments were conducted on individuals whose corpus callosum had been bisected. One of these tests examined responses to visual stimulation. While the patient fixed his gaze on

a central point on a board, spots of light were flashed for a tenth of a second in a row across the board that spanned both the left and the right half of his visual field. The patient was asked to tell what he had seen. Each patient reported that lights had been flashed in the right half of the visual field. When the lights were flashed only in the left half of the field, however, the patients generally denied having seen any lights.

Since the right side of the visual field is normally projected to the left hemisphere of the brain and the left field to the right hemisphere, one might have concluded that in these patients with divided brains the right hemisphere was, in effect, blind. We found, however, that this was not the case when the patients were directed *to point* to the lights that had flashed instead of giving a verbal report. With this manual response, they were able to indicate when lights had been flashed to the left visual field, and *perception with the brain's right hemisphere proved to be almost equal to perception with the left*. [Emphasis mine.]

Clearly, then, the patients' failure to report the right hemisphere's perception verbally was due to the fact that the speech centers of the brain are located in the left hemisphere.

You will note the observation that "one might have concluded that in these patients with divided brains the right hemisphere was, in effect, blind." This was *not* true.

This experiment proved that *you know a great deal that you cannot verbalize*. Since that time, many experiments have reinforced these first observations.

RIGHT BRAIN FRUSTRATION

If your intuitive communication system is not well developed, you may be making serious mistakes right now. Some important awareness of your right brain might not be properly transmitted and/or interpreted by your left brain. This failure often creates "right brain frustration," i.e., an unaccountable feeling of anxiety and helplessness, a feeling such as might come from seeing someone in great danger while in a foreign country and looking around desperately for a translator to help you because you don't know the language to warn them. You recognize the danger, know what to do, but there is no way to convey it. How upsetting when you know the person in danger is yourself.

This condition of right brain frustration accounts for much of the unhappiness, anxiety, and anger from which modern man suffers. Think of all the times you've felt depressed or angry and didn't know why. Think of all the times you felt like crying and could not account for it. Sometimes we desperately search for a reason and the left brain glibly supplies one, but we know deep down that the reason given is not the real cause of the malaise. We're just kidding ourselves.

Our two brains work together like a good doubles tennis team. Each of them can probably do everything required of a tennis player — serve, rally, volley, and so forth, but there is a tendency to specialize. Whenever the opportunity arises, they each take their own specialty. They constantly cover for each other. They help each other by yelling instructions and warnings to better coordinate the defense and attack necessary to achieve the common goal. Now, imagine one of the players is "mute." This player is like the right brain. The "mute" player sees many things his partner misses — and tries desperately to alert him, to warn him, to guide him — but if he can't get his partner's attention or make his message clear, the team will not succeed.

Just as tennis partners learn to communicate without talking — a pointed finger indicates direction, a palm facedown means the ball will bounce safe — you must learn to heed the nonverbal messages of your right brain. Whatever you can do to implement the flow of information between the two teammates helps develop better teamwork between them.

WHAT WILL INTUITIVE POWER DO FOR YOU?

I feel I have developed my mind in such a way that I can quickly assimilate and analyze data, and reach conclusions that are beyond rational explanation. That is a faculty that every successful politician must have if he is to be decisive. I believe I have a well-honed right side of the brain and my use of it might be defined by some as intuition.
— Edwin Edwards, Governor of Louisiana

Developing your intuitive skills will make a difference in your success, your happiness, your creativity, and your decision-making ability. Here are some of the ways that my students have benefitted from reaching their intuitive self. When you learn to use your intuitive system on a conscious level, these benefits will be yours as well.

1. *You will become more aware of your deep aspirations, your real potential, and your true goals.* Without intuitive input you are operating on less than all the information you need. You are like an eight-cylinder motor that is operating on only four cylinders. If you have never used your full intuitive potential to aid your coping process, you have no idea of your true abilities. How can you set goals for yourself when you don't have a true assessment of your ability?

2. *You will become more in touch with your essential self, with that which is unique about you as an individual.* When you open yourself up to your intuitive databank, you discover new aspects of your inner self. If you have suppressed your intuitive voice until now, you are functioning only on superficial awareness.

3. *You will perceive the significance of muddled situations more quickly.* The intuitive system is an extra sensing phenomenon. Its use brings additional information to that of the conscious five senses. It is amazing how effective just a

little more information can be in deciphering the whole picture. Do you remember the picture puzzle you enjoyed as a child in which you had to draw lines from one numbered dot to another? As you drew, a shape or form would suddenly appear, and you could recognize it as a bird or a tree. How much faster you could see the picture if some of the dots were connected before you started. Intuition will "connect the dots" of the muddled situations in your life.

4. *You will be able to read people's characters more accurately and promptly.* The intuitive system brings holistic awareness to the fore and sees things that are missed or overlooked by conventional awareness. The intuitive is not taken in by outward appearance, the trappings of wealth, fame, good looks, position, or status. It picks up signals that are not apparent and integrates them with others from the conscious system into a more realistic assessment of a person. Your intuitive sense is an invaluable "bullshit detector."

5. *You will become more aware of your personal needs, whether they involve hunger, sleep, boredom, work, play, or sex.* The intuitive system functions when you are awake and asleep. When you develop your intuitive skills, you open up channels of internal communications. You will be better able to identify needs that are not being met and to deal with the frustrations that are caused by them.

6. *You will improve your decision-making ability.* Intuition provides unconscious information that makes decision making easier and more reliable. You will make better decisions faster when you learn to trust your intuition.

7. *You will find the courage to act on your decisions.* As your decisions prove to be more effective, you will acquire more confidence in your decision-making ability. With confidence comes the courage to act. This is a learning process: We repeat the things that turn out right and avoid the others. When you do something successfully and repeat it often

enough, it becomes automatic, and the anxiety that is part of making a decision is dissipated.

8. *You will be able to improve your relationships with those important to you.* All our relationships with others depend on how we perceive their actions and attitudes toward us. You may be so habituated to your nearest and dearest that your conscious mind overlooks barely perceptible signals of pain or need. Developing and using your intuitive system makes you more sensitive to the needs of your loved ones.

9. *You will know better what to do in difficult situations.* Knowing what to do often depends on perceiving what the problem is. Albert Einstein said, "It is more important to know what the problem is than to find the solution because stating the problem correctly often leads almost automatically to the solution." Your intuition can clue you into both problem and solution — if you learn to tune into it and use it.

10. *You will know better how to fulfill your own needs.* Just as intuition makes it easier to pinpoint what your true needs are, it also facilitates the fulfillment of those needs. The intuitive system with its own storehouse of information and knowledge has an awareness of your special needs that are never verbalized. When you learn to bring this knowledge into consciousness you are able to fulfill those needs. The confidence of knowing yourself fully will give you the courage to take the steps necessary to change your life to suit yourself.

2

How Intuitive Are You?

To a greater or lesser degree, all humans are intuitive, since all are born with a left brain and a right brain. The prime measure for intuitive difference between one person and another is how *fully* each *uses* intuition in his daily life.

Is your intuitive input an important factor in your personal relations and decision making? Or are you solely directed by "reason and logic"? Are you aware of your feelings? Are you impulsive or deliberate? Do you feel good about the decisions you make? Do you recognize what's good for you? — and what isn't?

I have designed a quiz that will give you further clues about your intuitive quotient. It will not reflect a definitive measurement of your intuitive potential; there is no precise testing device for this. It is intended, rather, to give you some idea of how you rate on the intuitive scale and also to serve as a measure of your progress as you become more in touch with your intuitive system through the exercises in this book.

In developing the test, I owe much to two scientists who

worked on this aspect of psychology: Dr. E. Paul Torrance of the Department of Education Psychology at the University of Georgia, whose specialty is educational testing, and Dr. Malcolm Westcott, whose book *The Psychology of Intuition* reflects his extensive research on the subject. He defines intuitive people as "persons who require far less than normal explicit information to reach correct solutions to problems." Dr. Torrance developed tests to determine whether a subject is predominately a right brain learner or a left brain learner; Dr. Westcott designed tests to select people who meet his definition of intuitive.

I am also indebted to Dr. Donald E. Payne of Oxtoby-Smith, Inc., specialists in motivational research, who generously advised me about questionnaire techniques for uncovering the true motivation of the test-taker.

Record your answers with either a *Y* for "Yes" or *N* for "no" on a separate piece of paper (so your friends or family may also take the test without being influenced by your answers). There is no time limit; there are no trick questions. Simply record your first reaction to each question.

After you have finished reading the book and have practiced the exercises, I urge you to take the test again. There will undoubtedly be a significant change in your score.

TEST YOUR INTUITIVE QUOTIENT

1. Can you handle many things happening at the same time?
2. Do you like to improvise?
3. Do you have a strong moral sense?
4. Can you read body language?
5. Do you like to use analogies?
6. Do you prefer geometry to algebra?
7. Do you learn better by listening rather than performing or doing?

8. Do you have trouble understanding what a pet dog or cat is trying to tell you?
9. Do you have a happy sex life?
10. Are you a "winner" rather than a "loser"?
11. Has there been a significant change in your interests or likes in the past few years?
12. Do you make people laugh easily?
13. Are you better at remembering people than their names?
14. Do you have a "consuming passion"?
15. Do you enjoy skiing or mountain climbing?
16. Do you rely on your personal experience rather than the facts in making judgments?
17. Are you more serious than playful when you work on a problem?
18. Do you get along well with very young children?
19. Do you often express yourself by gestures or grimace?
20. Do you battle for lost causes?
21. Do you like to try new ways to do things?
22. Do you live life to the hilt?
23. Do you try to be yourself at all costs?
24. Do you like to take chances?
25. Are you happier when you know exactly what is going to happen?
26. Do you think better when you're lying down?
27. Do you feel good about yourself?
28. Do you express yourself by the way you sing, dance, or play?
29. Do you prefer to learn things you can use immediately?
30. Are you demanding?
31. Are you close to your family?
32. Are you interested in your dreams?
33. Do you follow your hunches?
34. Are you very confident?
35. Do you have wide emotional swings?
36. Do poetry and art really help you understand life?
37. Do you daydream a lot?
38. Do you usually know how people really feel about you?
39. Are you moved by emotional appeals?

40. Do you wait to see how you feel about something before making a decision?
41. Do you have trouble remembering emotions experienced in the past?
42. Are you spontaneous?
43. Do you prefer easy challenges to complex ones?
44. Are you able to perceive sizes and shapes correctly?
45. Are you often on the very edge of socially acceptable behavior?
46. Are you able to understand your emotions easily?
47. Do you prefer reading analytical works to reading fiction?
48. Are you good at knowing what will comfort a sick person?
49. Do you prefer logical solutions to problems rather than intuitive ones?
50. Has there been anyone in your life who has been particularly influential?

For answers, see page 19.

PROFILE OF THE HIGHLY INTUITIVE PERSON

From his research Dr. Westcott has formulated a profile of intuitive people:

- They are confident and unconventional problem solvers.
- They like reading and music and are deeply concerned with the big abstract questions like truth, beauty, and human values.
- They have strong belief in themselves.
- They are active in support of the things in which they believe.
- They take chances and believe you must take chances to get the most out of life.
- Though more self-reliant than average, they acknowledge being strongly influenced by other people in their careers and views.
- They are not afraid to make major changes in their lives.

- They are alert, demanding, confident, foresighted, informal, resourceful, spontaneous, and independent.

Intuitive people do have some negative characteristics, however:

- They often show a lack of social skills and social confidence.
- They are often uncomfortable in the limelight.
- They rarely feel good in any position of social initiative

This is, of course, a description of intuitive people in general. Characteristcs related to intuitiveness vary from person to person and from time to time as the individual develops and matures. You may want to speculate on the intuition quotient of each of your friends and members of your family. Select, if you can, the ones who are most intuitive, and consider what characteristics they have in common. It is likely you will find a high correlation with Dr. Westcott's profile.

ANSWERS TO TEST

1. Yes	9. Yes	16. Yes	23. Yes	30. Yes	37. Yes	44. Yes
2. Yes	10. Yes	17. No	24. Yes	31. Yes	38. Yes	45. Yes
3. Yes	11. Yes	18. Yes	25. No	32. Yes	39. No	46. Yes
4. Yes	12. Yes	19. Yes	26. Yes	33. Yes	40. Yes	47. No
5. Yes	13. Yes	20. Yes	27. Yes	34. Yes	41. No	48. Yes
6. Yes	14. Yes	21. Yes	28. Yes	35. Yes	42. Yes	49. No
7. No	15. Yes	22. Yes	29. Yes	36. Yes	43. No	50. Yes
8. No						

To arrive at your score, give yourself two points for each answer that is the same as the key. If you scored:

Between 90 and 100: You may think of yourself as highly intuitive. You accept and use intuitive input fully in coping with life and are able to enjoy a happier, better-adjusted life than most people.

Between 70 and 90: You are above average in intuitiveness, with a good working arrangement between the logical and the intuitive. There is room for improvement, which will come with greater confidence and application of the ideas in the book.

Between 50 and 70: You are not living up to your intuitive capacity. Working on the exercises described in the book will help you to free your intuitive voice and to accept its validity. You need to be encouraged to trust your intuition and use it.

Between 30 and 50: You are probably very logical, careful, and well organized. You may be the high-level product of our formal didactic educational system. Awakening your intuitive abilities will make a tremendous difference in your life.

Between 0 and 30: You are a predominantly left brain thinker. You have strong drives to conform and get things right. Your intuitive voice has been almost completely stifled. You should make every effort to develop new ways of thinking to add intuitive perception to your deliberations.

3

How to Recognize an Intuitive Signal

You receive intuitive messages every day of your life. Like a gigantic computerized telephone switchboard, the brain processes millions of messages each day, but with all the frenzied activity, it is difficult for intuitive signals to get through to your conscious awareness. Understanding what stands in their way is the first step toward tapping this essential personal resource.

WHY INTUITIVE MESSAGES DON'T GET THROUGH

1. Intuition is expressed in a language that is nonverbal. The right side of the brain, to which intuitive information is directed, does not use a rational process to arrive at its conclusions. Its understanding is holistic, arrived at through your feelings, moods, dreams, fantasies, reveries, and in personal images and symbols. Even when you are conscious of these feelings, you may tend to overlook their significance. The language of intuition must be decoded to be understood. And although many sensations and reactions may seem universal, each person's idiom is unique.

2. *The intuitive message is obscure.* An intuitive message must be put into an understandable context. The five senses are highly trained reporters: Their messages go directly to the brain, where they are instantly recorded, checked, and interpreted. For example, the temperature goes down; the skin sends a "cold" message and you button up your coat or move into the house where it's warmer. The intuitive message, however, is fragmentary like a piece from a jigsaw puzzle that must be fitted into the entire picture to make sense.

3. *We are not usually expecting the message.* It is easier to find something when you are looking for it. The five senses get results in part because they are almost always poised, ready to receive anticipated signals — the fragrance of a flower, noise of a motor, taste of lemon, and the like. There is generally no such alertness for messages from your intuitive because you have been conditioned to discount it. So even when the intuitive is clanging away, loud and clear, trying to signal you, you may not always pick up its message because it's often completely out of context with your conscious activity.

4. *The intuitive signal is usually very faint and ephemeral.* Unless an emotion or feeling is strong, you tend to ignore it, like a parent who pays attention to his child only when the child makes a fuss. I like to think that intuition is analogous to the signals sent out by the Count of Monte Cristo, who desperately tapped out his SOS on the wall of his dungeon; it was very faint, almost inaudible, but it was finally picked up by another prisoner, who wondered, "What can that tapping mean?" You can receive more and better intuitive information when you listen to yourself very closely.

5. *There is usually no logical evidence to support the intuitive message at the time you receive it.* Intuitive knowledge can be disturbing and unwelcome to the conscious mind. It may not fit into a logical method of problem solving. Intui-

tion is a threat to the conventional way of acquiring information: We have been trained to treat with deep suspicion any information that is not supported by concrete evidence. We tend to dismiss intuitive knowledge as trivial, frivolous, or inconsequential.

THE EXPERIENCE

A teacher can only be a guide, coach, or cheerleader. Only you can teach yourself! All the explanations in the world — all the yelling, drilling, exercises, and homework — are wasted on the closed mind. Only self-revelation works! Your knowledge grows from a series of insights that are intuitive revelations.

You can explain to nonswimmers a thousand times that there's no need to be afraid, that water will support the body, that if you take your feet off the ground and gently lie on the water, you will float. You can use blackboard diagrams, pictures, explanations of the physical properties of water and matter, and so forth. But it is only when the student gets into the water himself and summons the courage to experience what it's like, to trust himself on the water . . . yes, to give himself up to the water, that he ever knows what you're talking about. Once this sensation of floating is experienced and enjoyed, swimming is only a matter of time and development.

Intuitive awareness is like floating. It must be experienced. Once you recognize the sensation of intuition, once you are aware of it, you can build on it. It will truly become your sixth sense.

Like swimming, intuitive awareness is an experience that improves with confidence. A feeling of security and faith in what you're doing makes it possible. The speed at which you move from floating to swimming varies with the individual; so do the range and power of each person's intuitive sense.

Trial and error is a very basic way of learning, the fundamental way of acquiring first knowledge. The very first awakening of consciousness buds from trial and error and intuition. When a newborn meets the outside world, it is beset by thousands of messages relayed by the senses. What do they mean? Slowly, by constant trial and error, there is awareness and recognition. The infant learns to eat, to move toward warmth and security, and to cry for help. As time and knowledge grow, the process becomes more complex, but the exploring trial and error method continues all our lives. Strange how quickly many of us get discouraged when we use this learning fundamental to develop the intuitive sense.

To recognize intuitive signals and make them work for you requires trial and error. You must build a path for the intuitive.

BUILDING THE INTUITIVE PATH

Did you ever make your way through a wood or forest? The first time it is very hard. There are dozens of decisions to make. Is it best to go around that big tree? Should I step over this stream? Will going up over that mound make the trip any easier? Eventually you get through. The next time you make the trip, you recognize more of the landmarks and you solve many logistical problems in the same way. In some instances, you remember that the decision did not work out so well, so you try a new way. After you've made the trip several times, you will have worked out the best route. Soon you go down the path without thinking about what to do when you reach the tree or the stream. The strange, new, difficult way has become a path — easy to find, easy to follow. As time goes on, the path becomes a road — wider, more clearly defined, self-evident. Going across that wood becomes an automatic trip, almost a reflex. As a matter of fact, it becomes difficult to leave the road — you've made it into a groove!

THE QUESTION THAT UNLOCKS

The language of intuition consists of (1) feelings, (2) symbols, and (3) dreams. These provide the clues that will determine your intuitive path.

How can you figure out what your intuition is trying to tell you by your feelings, symbols, or dreams? An exercise I have used in my classes for many years is so simple that I am always concerned that it will not be taken seriously. I call it the "Intuitive Key." It consists of one word, yet it is a most effective method for unlocking the vast treasure-house of intuitive knowledge that everyone has. That word is *why*. When you experience a feeling you can't account for, stop and ask yourself — "WHY?" "Why do I feel this way?"

If you were faced with a maniacal-looking man running toward you with a bloody knife in his hand, you certainly would not have to ask yourself why you had a sudden feeling of terror. But if you get exactly the same feeling of terror during a job interview, asking "Why?" could be a most important question. And, just as important is sticking to the question and concentrating on your feelings — following them down any path they may take.

This "Why?" exercise should be used whenever you have a feeling you can't pin down to a rational cause. Repeat it. Keep asking "Why?" until you have an answer that you recognize is correct. You will know when you have the right answer: There will be a reaction in your body as well as your mind, a clicking into place, an illumination that suddenly makes everything clear. This is called the "Aha!" effect by psychologists, and it is a recognized phenomenon of recognition or insight.

When you ask "Why?" can also be important. Asking yourself "Why?" in the proper circumstances, when your emotions are calm and when you have time to think gives the intuitive system a chance to make itself heard. As you become more proficient in probing your intuitive system, you may find that eventually the intuitive will furnish your answer without your having to ask "Why?"

The "Why?" technique should be used for uncovering the meaning of feelings and symbols in your life and also to unravel the messages in your dreams.

FEELINGS

I strongly believe in the validity of intuition as a guide to action, especially in imponderable, difficult situations. Many times I have made a decision I just "had a feeling" about. Usually these decisions turned out all right.

— Bill Clinton,
Governor of Arkansas

The first awareness most of us have of our intuitive system is usually a vague sense of discomfort. Something is amiss. If the feeling continues, we become increasingly uneasy. We then try to identify the feeling in familiar terms such as excitement, nervousness, impatience, pleasure, calm, euphoria, happiness, anger, fear, anxiety, fervor, joy, affection, hostility, sadness, dread, boredom, distrust, foreboding, or a combination of these sensations.

Every feeling you experience must have a cause — either rational or intuitive. When you have a feeling with no *apparent* cause, you should always look for an intuitive message!

Feelings or moods are the basic language of intuition: The intuitive creates or controls many of our emotional responses and is able to do this independent of and, indeed, in spite of the wishes of the logical mind.

Have you ever felt afraid although you knew that logically there was absolutely nothing to worry about? Have you ever felt anger you couldn't reasonably account for? Have you ever felt sad and alone when you were with a gathering of happy people? In each case, your intuitive system was undoubtedly trying to reach you.

FEELINGS AS AN INTUITIVE VOICE

The folklore about "women's intuition" is probably true. In our culture women are permitted to express their feelings more openly than men, who have generally been conditioned to stifle them. "Manly," strong, men do not cry, pine, or show they are lonely or nervous. These feelings are considered signs of weakness, and so men have been trained to block intuitive signals. Men are supposed to be rational, logical, and deal only with the facts. "The facts, m'am, just give the facts" was the phrase that identified a tough television detective for years.

Women, for generations denied equal education that might have given them training in methods of reason and logic, have had to rely to a greater extent on intuitive cues. They have also been free to use their signals to communicate. We can speculate that the intuitive system of women developed more fully than that of men out of necessity. Since they were not forbidden this kind of awareness, it became one of the great advantages of that sex.

But men also have the equipment to be intuitive: They deny themselves a vital source of information when they eschew their intuition on the grounds that it is not a firm, decisive, or respectable source of knowledge. Primitive man (and woman) used any information he could; intuition makes for survival.

I consider myself to be very much a hunch player; I often go with my gut, including at least one mighty important decision lately.
— Dan Rather, on the eve of replacing
Walter Cronkite as CBS anchorman

Here's an example of how a high-powered executive responded to his intuition in time to avoid a bad mistake. The president of a public corporation recently told me:

"The chairman of the board of our company had made some premature and indiscreet remarks publicly about a possible merger with another company. I was amazed — his action was way out of line and also hurt the possibility of the deal going through. I had worked on it for a long time. I decided to tell him how annoyed I was.

"I dialed him direct for privacy. When his secretary answered the phone, I had a sudden feeling of foreboding.

"I'm not a green kid fresh out of graduate school with an M.B.A. I've headed this company for twenty years, but I gave in to that intuitive feeling and hung up without saying a word. I sat at my desk for a long time and asked myself why I had that terrible feeling.

"Suddenly it dawned on me. I remembered that the chairman was head of the committee that was deciding whether to retire me or extend my contract. My telling him off would absolutely have meant my retirement. My intuition caught me just in time. My contract *was* renewed and, incidentally, I was able to work out the merger successfully anyway."

This executive's intuitive insight was holistic: It took an overview of the entire situation and cautioned him against an action that would have been harmful to his future. Although his phone call might have been justifiable from a good management viewpoint, it would have been disastrous for him personally. How often has your intuition helped you avoid action that would have been ruinous for you in the long run?

When people recall an intuitive experience it is usually some very important turning point or crisis in their lives. The significance of the occasion fixes the experience in their memory and so there is a tendency to think of the intuitive experience as a dramatic crucial event. This is not the whole truth. The intuitive system features in the minutiae of our lives too. It delivers messages on the most pedestrian matters — but that does not diminish its importance. The quality of our lives is made up of many small events.

One morning recently I had to run to catch the train, and in order to get to my usual midcar seat, I had to dash past others on the station platform. When I settled back in my seat to read my newspaper, I became aware of feeling a bit depressed. I began to explore; I asked myself "Why?" Something I ate? No. The headlines? No. Someone around me? No. I closed my eyes to concentrate more deeply and continued to ask myself the key question — "Why?"

An image of Barry R. appeared. Barry R. is an old friend and neighbor who had recently lost his job. I knew he was depressed and sensitive about his current plight. If he was on the train and I hadn't acknowledged him, he might think I had snubbed him.

My heart-heavy feeling lessened a bit. Why had Barry popped into my mind? I got up to search the train. Sure enough, seated in the opposite end of the car, Barry R. was buried in his newspaper. I tapped him on the shoulder and said, "Hi, how are you?" The pleased look on his face confirmed my intuition: He had seen me and had assumed that I was ignoring him as I ran past in my haste to get a seat.

Yet, I would testify under oath that I never saw him on the train when I first entered, not, that is, on a conscious level. But my intuitive knew what my conscious had missed and called it to my attention. When I returned to my seat, my mood had completely lifted and I felt good.

SYMBOLS

The intuitive system expresses its message in puns, allegories, and symbols.

A symbol correlates to something else by resemblance,

association, or convention. It is a representative for a more basic element. We are surrounded by symbols and use them every day: trademarks, religious signs, music notes. In fact, the letters we use to write words are symbols for sounds, and the sounds are symbols for objects or for complicated ideas.

When the intuitive uses symbols, it is often very inventive. It uses them to try to reach your conscious by any means possible. To understand the message behind the symbol, you must look for the association or relevance. This is not as difficult as it sounds.

Keeping a written log of your dreams and random thoughts is a great help in understanding your intuitive signals and in interpreting your own symbols.

Example 1
Sylvia Plath wrote in *The Bell Jar:*

> I saw myself sitting in the crotch of this fig tree, starving to death just because I couldn't make up my mind which fig I would choose. I wanted each and every one of them, but choosing one meant losing all the rest, and as I sat there unable to decide, the figs began to wrinkle and go black, and one by one they plopped to the ground at my feet.

The tree, of course, was the symbol of her life, and the figs were the opportunities that she couldn't choose among and so eventually lost all.

Example 2
On Mother's Day, Donna S. received a box of chocolates from Harry, her husband, and her two grown children. That evening after she had done the dishes, she reached for the chocolates, but instead of opening the box, she felt a sudden surge of anger and threw the box into the garbage.

Surprised by her anger and her impulsive act, Donna sat down at the kitchen table and tried to figure them out. Donna had attended my class a year before, and she remembered the Intuitive Key: "Why?" Why was she angry for no apparent reason; why had she thrown the gift candy away?

It took some time but finally Donna had the "Aha!" response. She realized that for years she had felt unappreciated, unloved, and overlooked by her family. On many occasions candy had symbolized love to her. But the box of chocolates was an ersatz love, not the real appreciation she craved. When Donna threw out the chocolates, she was symbolically rejecting what she considered a poor substitute for love. She was in effect saying, "You don't give me the real love and appreciation I deserve, so I won't accept this symbol."

Donna received her intuition's early warning signal in time. When I last saw her, she was doing quite well. She had discussed her unhappiness with her family and they were quick to make amends. She was surely using her *conscious* mind to solve the problem. But if she had not stopped to try to understand the message behind her feelings and her unconscious symbolic act, she might never have identified the problem at all. She might still be brooding about her unhappiness.

OPENING THE COMMUNICATION CHANNELS

It is important to keep the communication channels open as wide as possible between the logical mind and the intuitive. One way to maximize this is through deep relaxation, which has been used in various forms in psychology, medicine, and religion. It is a safe, simple, and effective method to clear the mind, release muscular tension, and heighten your receptivity to any faint intuitive signals that come through. (It can also be used whenever you want to unwind, fall asleep, or contact your intuitive self for exploration.)

Here is an exercise designed to help you achieve relaxation and expand your responsiveness to intuitive input. Use it as a warm-up for each of the other exercises in this book.

BASIC WARM-UP

- Sit in a chair with your feet flat on the floor, arms at your sides, eyes closed, back straight.
- As you breathe, let all thoughts drop away.
- Concentrate on your breathing; shed all other thoughts and be aware only of your own breathing. Do not try to control it; observe it and in your mind closely follow the air as it enters your nostrils, moves up through the nasal passages, down into your throat, and then into your lungs.
- Notice how your chest and stomach expand as the air moves in, and then — as the air retraces its path — how your diaphragm contracts and pushes the air out of your mouth. Treat the inhaling and exhaling as a single cycle absorbing your total *relaxed* attention.
- Note how different parts of your body react as they relax and shut down. You may notice how uneven your breathing is and how hard it is to concentrate on your breathing without trying to control it.
- It may also be difficult to keep your mind from wandering. Many find it is easier to concentrate on the breathing by making a note of the number of inhale-exhale cycles completed. Set a goal of fifty or even one hundred cycles. You will usually be totally relaxed and in a sort of twilight zone, ready to let subtle feelings and fleeting visions pass through your half-awake mind.
- If you don't achieve this state in the first try, extend the number of breathing cycles you set as your goal.

Why don't you try it right now!

Simple as this is, it is an effective way to achieve deep relaxation without danger or harmful side effects. Once you have learned how to achieve this "twilight zone" state, you can move on to exercises that reach for designated goals.

The following exercise is designed to help you search out the faintest intuitive input for a *specific* problem. It is not necessary that you do everything in the order described here.

You may discover variations that are faster or more effective for you. Use them. All the exercises are exploratory learning experiences.

THE INNER PILOT

1. Select a problem, decision, or choice you are facing. Do not select a major problem, since you are just starting; rather, choose something that is merely bothersome. Write a simple statement that describes it.
2. Choose a room that is fairly insulated from sound and light. Lie on a firm couch or bed; if necessary, lie on a blanket on the floor. The temperature should be comfortable enough for you to wear nothing but pajamas or a loose gown. No shoes, stockings, wristwatch, or glasses. Do everything necessary to eliminate all external stimuli. Lie face up and shut your eyes.
3. Focus on the problem you've selected. Run through all the arguments pro and con. Examine them in all their possible dimensions. Consider all the nuances of the problem and mentally follow through the possible consequences of every solution.
4. Go into the Basic Warm-up and allow all directed thought to slip away. Concentrate on your breathing and pay close attention to how you feel as images come into your mind.
5. Now turn over each possible solution and its consequence again, using as little conscious direction as possible. Do not interfere with your body's tendency to cooperate. You will discover perceptible shades of feeling connected with each solution, and then gradually (or suddenly), you will become aware that you feel better about one of them. You feel more relaxed, more at ease as you consider it. You may be surprised to find new reasons why that particular choice seems to be the best one. You will feel "good" about the choice, and it will seem to you that it is the only choice to make: *You will have had your intuitive message.*

This exercise is excellent for building confidence in your intuition. In time, this confidence and your internal reorientation will make it possible for you to recognize an intuitive message instantly.

Because of its simplicity many people will say, "That's not intuition — all you did was think about the problem in a relaxed way." But that's exactly how the intuitive works. When the left brain relaxes its dominance of your awareness, the intuitive message can get through. It acts as a pilot, steering and guiding your conscious mind.

4

The Message in
Your Dreams

Peter, a fifty-one-year-old insurance salesman, awoke one morning from a dream so vivid he couldn't wait to tell his wife about it. In the dream, he and his wife, Kate, fifty, were strolling on the beach. Peter looked down and suddenly noticed that Kate was in the seventh or eighth month of pregnancy. He was astonished and chided her for having kept it a secret for such a long time. Kate answered that she hadn't revealed it to him because she didn't want to worry him.

When Peter told his wife about the dream that morning while they were still in bed, she laughed and commented, "Wouldn't it be wonderful to be young enough to get pregnant again!"

But Peter had a residual uneasiness, the same feeling he had when he had awakened from the dream, and he couldn't think of any reason for his mood. With his dream in his mind, he looked over at Kate as she slipped into her bathrobe and noticed that the lower left side of her abdomen was slightly distended. Kate said she had not noticed it, but her clothes did seem to be getting tight. Peter insisted she see a doctor, and his examination revealed a large ovarian tumor. An operation was successful in removing the tumor, but Peter never forgot the doctor's postoperation words: "If we had let it go much longer, I don't think we could have saved her." Peter's dream had alerted them, and saved Kate's life. His intuitive system had noted what was not evident to his conscious mind.

SLEEP: WHEN THE UNCONSCIOUS REIGNS

Dreams are one of the important voices of the intuitive because the conscious mind is recessive in sleep and the non-verbal mind reigns.

As we have learned, the most favorable conditions for receiving intuitive messages are during periods of quiet and serenity, whenever the logical thinking apparatus is subdued or shut down. That is what happens in sleep.

Sleep creates the perfect opportunity for the intuitive to surface. The left brain is, for all intents and purposes, dormant during sleep and its judgmental faculties are not operative.

Sleep research has established that there are four levels of sleep, each level going further from wakefulness, until the fourth and deepest level, which is so deep that a bright light flashed directly at an open eye produces no reaction from the sleeper; at this level all five senses have been shut down, including vision.

But we do not stay in this deep sleep very long. After about ten minutes, we float from sleep stage to sleep stage until we start dreaming; some researchers have considered this yet another stage of sleep.

In most of us, short twenty-minute dream sequences occur at ninety-minute intervals. Finally, there seems to be a roundup dream that includes most of the others and lasts about an hour just before waking. If you ever awakened feeling you've had many dreams in one night, you probably have.

Dreams derive their material from reality, from that which we have experienced, read, seen, heard, or thought about. While the intellectual faculty (the left brain) suspends its action, the right brain, the intuitive, keeps right on "working over" problems that the left brain wrestled with during the day. Since the right brain is nonverbal, the receiving of the information takes place in scenarios that often unfold with awesome richness of detail.

The "distortion" in dreams is called, by some experts, the "dreamwork." The condensation, displacement, and representation of one thing by another may be ways by which the intuitive deals with sensitive material, which it disguises to make more acceptable to the left brain's judgmental faculties. Hence, there is no logic or reason in dreams. You can fly, walk through walls, catch a speeding bullet. Time passes quickly or slowly. People you know die, and dead people appear alive to you. You can have totally absurd dreams, or dreams of embarrassment (walking down Main Street without your trousers is a typical embarrassment dream) or of anxiety, fear, or joy.

The real meaning in your dreams must be deciphered by understanding the analogies or symbols. Your intuitive knows and understands the true meaning of your dreams because it creates them. When you fail to understand, the intuitive often repeats the dream or tries to convey the same message in a different way, like a teacher working with an inattentive student.

Why are dreams forgotten more readily than, say, the plot of an adventure movie, or even the phone numbers you dial infrequently, which seem to stick in your mind with no effort at all? The same causes that lead to forgetting things in waking life operate for dreams as well. When we are awake we overlook countless things we've perceived because they were too weak in intensity to be remembered or because the "mental excitation" attached to them was too slight, or because we don't think they are of any relevance.

Second, dreams, in most cases, lack logical development and orderliness, which makes them hard to remember. (Though, conversely, the more peculiar the dream, the more likely you are to remember it.) The dreamwork, puns, and symbols that make dreams hard to decipher, also causes us to forget them.

A third reason we forget dreams is that the moment we wake up the conscious world impinges on us with a vengeance. As we move from sleep into wakefulness, the left brain takes over and seems to shout to the five senses, "Everybody up, up, up!"

Last, and most important for us: Dreams are forgotten because most people take very little interest. They view their dreams gingerly, with trepidation and treat them like Pandora's box.

IMPROVING YOUR DREAM RECALL

In order to use your intuition to understand your dreams — to intuit your dreams — you must first of all improve your ability to recall the dreams in detail.

Welcome to the Magic Theater, a handbook for exploring dreams, by Dick McLeester, points up a most appropriate analogy: We are the "writers, producers, directors, and stars of our own dreams. We are also the audience."

To be more specific, your right brain is the writer, producer, and director, and the scenario is your experiences, problems, fears, hopes, and wishes. A wealth of information lies dormant in your right brain, only to come out at night and parade upon the stage of your sleeping mind. Someone once said that a dream can be compared to a magnificent firework, which goes off in a moment but which took hours, days, or even weeks to prepare.

How can you lasso this production and record it vividly in your consciousness so that you can probe it for meaning? Here are some techniques to help you:

1. *Making up your mind before you go to sleep to remember your dreams is very effective.* Having a "receptive mental set" is important. Just thinking "Remember tonight's dream!" before sleep can produce results. You are, in effect, programming your conscious to remember in much the same way many people can program themselves to wake up at a certain time. No one knows why this works, but it does work for many people. Some scientists are known to take mathematical problems to bed in order to "sleep on them," and there are reports, perhaps apocryphal, of solutions "miraculously" arrived at in the morning.

2. *Keep a pencil and pad always at your bedside.* There are pens with lights in their points if you have a sleeping partner whom you do not want to disturb. *You must write down your dreams* if you wish to interpret them. It is frustrating to remember you had a tremendously important dream, to feel the full intensity of its emotions, but to lack any recall — to have not the slightest clue to the actual images.

3. *Record the dream immediately upon awakening.* Once you are awake enough to realize you have had a dream, the dream should be noted, even if you wake up in the middle of the night. You need not write the dream in full detail, but include enough to jog your memory in the morning. Sometimes the vision you select to note will be the essence of the message in your dream.

4. *Recall and record the dream as though it is happening in the present.* For example, your recalled script should read: "I enter a large beautiful room. It has green walls and there is

music. As I move toward the stairs, I see a man standing in the shadows. He waves at me."

HOW NOT TO INTERPRET DREAMS

Interpreting a dream has come into disrepute in the past, with psychics, fortune-tellers, and gypsies getting into the act. Indeed, from the earliest times people have tried to interpret dreams by two basic methods. I mention these only in passing because they are to be avoided:

1. *Prophetic dream interpretation.* An example of this is the pharaoh's dream, which was interpreted by Joseph in the Bible: "The seven fat kine followed by seven lean kine that ate up the fat kine" was interpreted by Joseph to mean that seven years of famine would consume all that was produced in seven years of plenty. This was actually a *prophecy* on Joseph's part, and though it may demonstrate how clever he was in discerning weather trends and how long the stored food might last, it doesn't qualify as genuine dream interpretation.

Since dreams are based on our past experiences, they can only elucidate the past for us. At most, we can hope that they will aid us to make wise decisions in the future, based on our true feelings, but that is all. Do not look for your dream to foretell the sex of your unborn child or whether you will win the state lottery.

2. *The decoding method.* This method employs a "dream book," which purports to give you the real meanings of certain recurring symbols or situations in dreams. For example, if you were to look up "wedding" in the dream book, you may find it symbolizes death; or a funeral in your dream may symbolize good luck. There is no rhyme or reason to this method, and the symbols assigned to each thing have no basis in fact. Symbols are unique to each individual. Only *you* can determine what a particular thing in your dream means to *you*.

READING YOUR DREAM MESSAGES

Here is an exercise that will help you unravel the message in your dreams:

1. Lie down in a darkened, quiet room where you will have minimum intrusion from stimuli to the five conscious senses.

2. Shut your eyes and go into the Basic Warm-up (see page 32).

3. Feel yourself gliding into a deep relaxation. The state is similar to the drowsy feeling prior to falling asleep. But do not worry about whether you achieve this state or not — if you are close, it is sufficient.

4. Program yourself to abandon all critical and judgmental thought. Your mind should float, touching on no particular subject.

5. Repeat to yourself that you are now abandoning all critical and judgmental capacity. You are going to let all ideas play into your mind, good or bad, and you will accept them all on equal footing. When you are judgmental, you activate left brain participation and crowd out the intuitive. Allow ideas and visions to emerge freely. Do not try to direct your thoughts.

6. Take any portion of the dream you want to interpret and observe what pops into your mind. Let the visions and mental pictures unfurl, roll around on your twilight-sleep screen; do not make any judgments.

7. Try another portion of your dream. Follow the same procedure and repeat, until you have gone through the whole dream considering each vision, thought, and emotion that comes to your mind.

8. Be receptive to the "Aha!" effect. As you go through the steps above, notice the sudden insights that may arise at different points, revealing part or all of the dream message. Hold on to them. Stop and savor each one, let them sink in with all their implications.

HELEN B.'S DREAM ANALYSIS

Let us now take a sample dream and see how it was intuitively analyzed by the above method. Several years ago, Helen B. described a recurring dream thus:

> I am in a huge brick building of several stories, with many doors and windows. Every few feet there is another door. I go from door to door, trying each doorknob and rattling the door, but none of the doors will open. I feel anxious and afraid.

This is how Helen B. analyzed the dream after going through the preliminary relaxation steps:

I am in a huge brick building of several stories. . . . "It looked like a college, or an institution of some sort. I remember that my elementary school looked something like that, with the same red bricks. It was an oppressive building, with bars on the windows, and I hated it — I always felt oppressed and locked in there."

With many doors and windows . . . "The elementary school had many windows but not so many doors. I remember wishing it had many doors so we could get out faster."

Every few feet there is another door . . . "The door has always represented an exit for me. An escape. It is a means of getting out."

I go from door to door . . . "Obviously, I am looking for an exit. I want to get out of that dreary institution."

But none of the doors will open . . . "There is no way out for me. I can find no way out of this oppressive prison building. I am trapped in it."

It was suggested Helen go back to the vision of the building again to figure out what it was, since this seemed the basic key to the meaning of the dream.

> *The building* . . . "It is an institution of some kind. Institutions are for orphans, education, the insane, the blind. The institution of marriage. Of course, my marriage!"

Helen had finally interpreted the dream, and its meaning came to her in a flash. She was looking for a way out of her marriage, which was as oppressive to her as elementary school had been in her childhood. The dream was one of her first clues that the trapped feeling she had came from her marriage.

JOAN'S DREAM

Joan, a writer, shares this dream, and her unraveling of it:

I am trying to fly above a crowd by flapping my arms. It is difficult and I am working very hard to get myself off the ground. Finally I get up in the air, start to take off, when someone in the crowd below grabs me by the ankle and tries to pull me down. Then another person grabs me and also tries to pull me down. I wake up in a sweat.

Using the intuitive method of dream analysis this is what she reported:

> *I am trying to fly above a crowd by flapping my arms.* . . . "I am trying to 'rise above the crowd' — I want so much to be a good writer. Flapping my arms, that could be typing. I guess I do sort of flap my arms when I'm working at my typewriter."

> *It is difficult and I am working very hard to get off the ground* . . . "I was having trouble with my novel, I couldn't get it started. I couldn't, literally, 'get it off the ground'!"

Finally I am up in the air, start to take off. . . . "I finally did get the novel going last month. I outlined the plot and wrote a first draft of two chapters."

When someone in the crowd grabs me by the ankles and tries to pull me down. . . . "I had shown a chapter to a friend and had got some rather adverse feedback. It was a real setback. I began to feel I could never write a good novel."

Then another person grabs me and also tries to pull me down. . . . "I had also shown a chapter to another friend, and she made several corrections that I thought were nit-picking."

Joan's "Aha!" came when she realized that in order to "rise above the crowd," she couldn't let herself become stalled by the comments of people whose motivation, her intuition told her, was not to help but to hold her back.

Did intuition help this author to finish writing the book? Two years later, Joan says, "I'm not sure, but after I analyzed that dream, I didn't show chapters to anybody. I just sat down and kept on writing until the book was finished."

You can compare dream interpretation to the party game of charades, in which one team is supposed to guess the title of a song, book, or movie while an opposing team acts out the words in letters or symbols. Your team may guess the first word of the title, then the last, and then finally someone may in a flash come up with the entire title. Dream interpretation is something like that: You get a hint here, another hint there, and finally it all comes to you in a flash in which it all makes sense, and you wonder why you didn't instantly realize what the dream meant.

Remember: You are the best person to interpret your dreams. Dreaming is one part of you trying to reach another part. A teacher or therapist may teach you the technique of analyzing dreams, but *you* are the only one who can determine the meaning of a dream symbol for you.

MISCONCEPTIONS ABOUT DREAMS

Alas, even to this day there are skeptics, those who claim that dreams are gibberish and best forgotten.

Ignore these skeptics; they are cut from the same cloth as those who could never believe that man would someday talk through a wire or reach the moon. Those of us who use intuition to its fullest cannot wait until science has conclusively proved that dreams are significant to us. There is enough evidence at present to encourage us to use this valuable source of feedback from our right brain.

Freud has in a way given dreams a bad name; by this I refer to the fact that he highlighted the importance of sex in dreams so that many people are fearful even today that their dreams will reveal their innermost secrets about sex. They do not dare to delve very deeply into their dreams; they feel uncomfortable and ashamed.

Recent studies in sleep laboratories, however, have concluded that only thirty percent of our dreams are concerned with sex. As we can see by the two dreams analyzed in this chapter, sex is not an obsessive component in dreams for today's post-sexual-revolution population. Nevertheless, since human sexuality is a normal part of our day-to-day concerns, you will probably confront your sexual self from time to time in your dreams; it is no more to be feared than confronting your work self or your interpersonal self.

INTUITIVE DREAMS SPEAK ON MANY LEVELS

A practicing therapist related this incident. A woman patient told of a recurring dream that always left her with a feeling of dread and foreboding. No matter how her dream started, it would always end with her driving a car with no brakes, careening down one of the high mountains in the area.

The therapist, who had treated the woman for some time and was familiar with her problems and the complexities of her life, pointed out that the whole episode represented the fact that she was falling in love with a married man. The restraints were being cast off one by one, and deep down she was afraid that it was all going too fast and she feared that it would end disastrously. She was very impressed, and after a long, searching session, the patient was able to make some plans for straightening out her life. The next session brought an astonishing sequel, however.

"You know, doctor," she began, "after our last talk, when you explained what my dream meant, I felt so relieved and good about everything. When I got back in my car and started over the mountain again, I thought about the dream, and it suddenly occurred to me that I should have my brakes checked. I pulled into the next gas station. You know the mechanic said they were so threadbare they might have gone anytime. He said, 'You could get killed driving with brakes like that!' "

Intuition had spoken on two levels: one symbolic, one factual. If a dream recurs over and over, you must suspect that your intuitive system is trying to make you aware of something important. Also, do not ignore dreams that involve strong feelings. Dreams and emotions are a voice of the intuitive; together they indicate that the intuitive is trying to reach you with an important message.

Do not be afraid of your dreams. If there is something terrifying in a dream, consider it an opportunity to examine what may be fearful for you in real life.

Many people who have nightmares and depressing dreams can be helped by opening up their intuitive systems. The better the interaction between the intuitive and the conscious, the less important are dreams, emotions, and the messages from them. When the intuitive system is bottled up, it is forced to find expression when the left brain dominance is quiescent in sleep. People who are very intuitive, who accept and rely on their intuition, do not have as many disturbing or significant dreams as those who suppress the intuitive voice.

There is a kind of dreaming called "lucid dreaming." This refers to the ability to have a dream and *know* that you are dreaming while you are still dreaming. You have the feeling of being on the outside looking in on yourself in the dream. If you are one of the lucky few who are able to achieve this, you may also be one of the few people who can hope to achieve "creative dreaming." This is the ability to guide your dream while in the act of dreaming — a phenomenon that is quite rare but can be learned. It is less common than being able to program what you are going to dream about by thinking of the subject at night or before sleeping. Apparently many people are able to influence their intuitive to dream about a predetermined topic. This interplay of the conscious and the intuitive during lucid dreaming — also called "creative dreaming" and "programmed dreaming" — makes for better cooperation between the two systems of awareness.

To end this chapter, I am including one of my own dreams, which I finally interpreted, and later confirmed. You'll be able to do this too — when you learn to use your intuition.

I am visiting relatives, where we are enjoying ourselves talking and eating. Suddenly a woman walks through the side of the house, right through the room, through us, and then disappears through another wall. We are surprised, but continue our conversation. A short while later, the woman appears again. This time she stops, glares at us, picks up a stool, and runs through the wall, with all of us in pursuit. We do not catch her and do not recognize who she is. I wake up feeling uneasy and a bit unhappy.

After going through the dream interpretation steps, I finally realized that the woman was undoubtedly my sister and the message was she felt I had been neglecting her. I had a great sense of relief when I realized what the dream meant, because I could easily rectify the situation. A few months later my sister did indeed tell me that she had been hurt by what she felt was my distant attitude toward her, and that she had been annoyed because I visited other relatives more often than I visited her.

A FEW LAST POINTS

Sometimes we overcomplicate the process of dream interpretation by looking for obscure allusions. Dreams are not always loaded with deep messages; they may be reminding you of nothing more complicated than that you must water your plants. When Freud said, "An unexplained dream is like an unopened letter," he had no idea of the amount of junk mail we get today!

Here is a word of encouragement. Don't expect to find the dream message in your first go-round. Work on it. Then stop for a while and come back to it. Your chances of interpreting it correctly are always increasing because your intuitive system is working on it too. Sooner or later the two systems will find a way.

5

Enticing Intuition

Now we shall try to entice the intuitive to play a more active role in your life.

You may find yourself resisting some of the intuition-supporting exercises in this chapter — particularly the sense-deprivation category — for a number of reasons:

The "it's too sensual" dodge: The sensuality of the exercise elicits resistance; relax and enjoy the pleasure of touching and feeling with unabashed joy.

The "it's too frightening" dodge: Although you may never have done anything comparable to the exercises, there is no actual risk involved. Count on your instincts to guide you.

The "it's too silly" dodge: Our residual fear of being foolish can stop you from doing something that might seem experimental or "frivolous." There doesn't have to be a "practical" motive in all our behavior. Each day you do much that can hardly be called practical.

The lazy "I'll-take-your-word-for-it" dodge: Don't just

read the exercise; you must try it yourself. Only by doing can you experience it. Reading about something is *not* the same as experiencing it.

The "I-already-knew-that, so-what-else-is-new" dodge: Allow yourself to savor the exercises, even if you have already experienced one or more of them. Don't just whiz by this section with a sense of being above it all. If you do, you are just cheating yourself.

Let me emphasize that the exercise experiences are carefully developed to reach the right brain. The actual experiencing of the exercises is what invokes your intuition; reading about them reaches only your left brain. Put yourself through each experience described at least once so that the nonverbal brain may experience the lesson *intuitively*.

It may help to practice the exercises in an Intuitive Consciousness-Raising Group with other people who are learning how to encourage their intuition. Such a group can provide not only a partner who is understanding, serious, and willing to go through the exercises with you, but also the emotional support and feedback so important to any learning situation. See the section in chapter 16, on how to form an Intuitive Consciousness-Raising Group.

THE TECHNIQUES

We know that the intuitive expresses itself through feelings, symbols, dreams, fantasy, or visions. By encouraging and developing these we open up the channels for better intuition.

Many of the following exercises will require you to begin by visualizing. That, however, does not mean the exercises are all the same. Visualization is the key that lets you in the door. What you find thereafter depends on where you go. Each exercise is aimed at a different target. Recall, recognition, and reminiscing all seem similar, but you can readily see they are different functions. For example:

Recall is the ability to remember a telephone number.
Recognition is the ability to recognize a face even thirty years later (after all those years of change).
Reminiscing is the ability to review in your mind events of long ago.

Here are four basic methods useful in nudging your intuitive to come forth with more clarity and in teaching you how to recognize barely perceptible signals:

1. Resonance
2. Judgment deferral
3. Sense deprivation
4. Forced decisions

Each exercise has been designed to make use of at least one of these methods.

THE RESONANCE EFFECT

Here's a new way to get in touch with gut-level feelings. Emotions are an important language of intuition. When you make certain vocal sounds, emotions "resonate" with them. That is, the sound produced helps "stir up" the emotion. The physical process of creating — and hearing — such sounds can awaken and expand the feeling that *resonates* with them. The dictionary says that to "resonate" means to produce a "vibration of large amplitude . . . by a relatively small stimulus" and that is what you will be doing. The small stimulus will be your vocalizations, and the emotions brought forth may prove to be of large enough amplitude to permit recognition and also meaningful intuitive insights.

In a somewhat similar way the Stanislavsky method of acting compels the actor to go back into his life to re-create the emotion that he is supposed to be portraying: A past incident in his life can spark the emotion he wishes to elicit. In the Resonance Exercise, you will draw upon an experience from your own life to awaken an emotion, but this time you will only perform vocally — in private and at a time of your own choosing. You will have the opportunity to associate your inner feelings with the sounds you will produce, so that when you *experience these feelings in the future*, you will recognize them and the intuitive messages they contain.

As you review the thoughts that surface during the exercise, you may uncover intuitive messages that you have suppressed for years. The vocal sounds may bring up images that are important clues to what provokes these emotions in you.

Select a relatively soundproof room where you will not be heard or disturbed. Since we are almost never insulated from hearing or being heard in our highly interrelated world, this is not easy to do. An ideal place is a car parked in a quiet spot with the windows rolled up and the motor off. Any noises outside the car need not be a distraction; they often fade into the background and become white noise.

This exercise should take not less than ten minutes and may last half an hour or more.

THE RESONANCE EXERCISE

1. Start with the Basic Warm-up. Close your eyes and concentrate on your breathing.
2. When you are completely relaxed, let your jaw drop and breathe through your mouth. Allow your vocal cords to aspirate, and at each succeeding exhalation add more intensity to the sound.
3. As the sound becomes a sob, make it louder and less re-

strained with each breath. Let it build until it is almost a howl, then a shriek, and ultimately a scream as piercing as you can produce. The sound should build as you become more and more uninhibited. Let yourself go. The ultimate shriek may be terrifying to anyone who could hear it — and perhaps even to you. Do not turn back. If you find that the sobbing tends to become wailing and the wailing produces tears, let it happen that way. Have a good cry. If the sobs turn to anger and become howls of rage, let them.

4.   With your eyes still closed, mentally note what happened to you. Are your hands and feet trembling? Do you have a feeling of terror or shock? Note your pulse and pounding heart. Do you feel tension in your stomach, or do you feel relief? What images are racing through your mind?

5.   When your breathing returns to normal, review the experience in your mind and recall what feelings you associated with the sounds you made. Look for the intuitive signals that this emotional experience invoked.

This exercise should not be confused with Primal Therapy screams. It does not purport to effect any therapy, as primal screaming ostensibly does; its function is to isolate and evoke specific feelings for you to note for future reference and insight.

THE SOUND OF MUSIC

This exercise is similar to the Resonance Exercise, except that instead of the sobs, you may make musical sounds on each exhalation in step two. As the sounds grow louder and take on characteristics of music or humming, allow yourself to sing. Whether it becomes a recognizable melody or a tune invented by you is not important. Listen to your song, then make observations of how you feel, what you are thinking, and what images come to your mind.

THE HAPPY SOUND

This time, instead of a sob or a musical sound, allow the sounds to become a giggle or a chuckle. At each succeeding exhalation, in step two, let the chuckle build until it is a laugh. Let yourself go, enjoy your laughter as it builds. After it subsides, make careful observations of how you felt and about what you fantasized. You may develop new insights about what, or *who,* makes you feel happy.

The Resonance effect is a remarkable way to help you do what you should have done a long time ago: understand what your feelings mean. Just as you need to know what words mean to comprehend thoughts and ideas, so you must know what each feeling means to grasp the intuitive awareness.

JUDGMENT DEFERRAL

Alex Osborne developed "brainstorming" as a technique to help business and creative advertising agencies generate new ideas about specific topics. Each person in a brainstorming session spins off every idea that comes to mind, no matter how fantastic, far-out, or inapplicable — and all are accepted and recorded with equal weight. Ideas flourish. *All evaluation of the ideas is postponed until the session is over.* No one is allowed to say, "No, that won't work," "We tried that last year," or "That's a crazy idea."

The production of ideas is separated from their evaluation because *judgment and evaluation inhibit the production of new ideas.*

Judgment also stifles intuition. If you can suspend judgment about whatever pops into your mind during an intuition-evoking exercise, you give free rein to the intuitive.

The following exercises require that you postpone judgment during the process. Try at least once and do it slowly. If you rush through them, you may miss a vital component: the head-clearing sense of relaxation so important to intuitive receptivity.

It is important, however, to have time immediately after each exercise to review your thoughts while the experience is still fresh in your mind. One of the disadvantages of trying to do the "Music Hath Charms" Exercise at a live concert is that when the music stops, the lights go up, people move about, and the intuitive mood is disrupted. One way of dealing with this is to close the reverie before the music stops and allow yourself enough time for the mental review before the lights go up.

"MUSIC HATH CHARMS" EXERCISE

You've probably done this simple exercise in one way or another countless times but never associated it with increased receptivity to your intuition: listening to classical music. A quartet by Mozart or Haydn works best for some people, but almost any instrumental music except overly familiar popular or dance forms will do. Set the volume a bit lower than usual for you, and proceed:

1. Close your eyes, suspend judgment, stop all directed thought, and simply listen.
2. After a while, permit the music to become background sound. Do not concentrate on the sound or what it is saying to you. Allow your fantasies full play. Become an outside observer, noting what is happening inside you, but do not direct your thoughts.
3. The first time you do this exercise, you may be inclined to stop too soon. Let the fantasy/music/dream continue for the entire length of the piece, if possible.
4. Afterward, review the experience, particularly the imagery that drifted through your mind and the feelings you experienced while you listened. What do these images mean to you? How do they bear on any problems or decisions you are facing?

It isn't unusual for a solution to a problem to occur to you during this exercise even though you hadn't intended to look for one. The dynamic is, your intuitive system has had a chance to provide input about a problem it was considering.

Many other situations can provide a restful, mind-clearing opportunity to reach intuition. Here are a few that may work for you.

WAVE WATCHER

Sitting at the seashore, looking at the sea, try "gazing" rather than looking. Listen for the lapping of the waves. Breathe for deep relaxation with eyes open or closed. Try to get a feeling for the infinity of life as encompassed in the eternal motion of the sea. Some people virtually become mesmerized watching the rhythmic movement of the waves. In this state of peaceful observation, your intuition has an opportunity to be heard.

SKY GAZER

Lying in a hammock, gaze at the sky and the lazy, slow-moving clouds. The gentle swaying of the hammock and the whisper of breezes can create a restful atmosphere that helps the intuitive to surface.

WARM FLOATER

Ease gently into a hot bath until you are totally submerged except for your face. Concentrate on total relaxation as you experience the sensual pleasure of floating aimlessly in warm water. Allow all directed thought to leave your mind. Close your eyes, float, and listen as the intuitive takes center stage.

PASSENGER PAUSE

When you are on a long trip, time need not be wasted. Look out the window at the passing scene. Allow your conscious tension to fall away. Focus on your breathing, relax, and permit random thoughts to float through your mind. Defer all judgment of the thoughts. The drone of the motor or the whine of wheels on the road or the clacking of train wheels can serve as soothing background white noise while you permit the intuitive to dominate.

SENSE DEPRIVATION

Your brain and five senses have your survival as their first priority. By cutting off or limiting one of your five senses, you force the other senses to work harder to compensate for the loss — and to accept help of the intuitive.

In these exercises, you will deliberately shut off one sense in order to experience the heightened alertness of the other four. You will discover that the intuitive system will come to your aid as well. You will experience a heightened input from the nonverbal mind as it tries to help you survive. There will be more unaccountable "knowing" as you cope.

THE SENSUOUS MEAL

This experience calls for the help of a willing and sensitive partner, and thus is particularly suitable for the Intuitive–Consciousness-Raising Group: You are going to eat a meal completely blindfolded and without conversation.

1. Choose a room conducive to an enjoyable experience, one with enough free space in the center of the room so that you can spread an old blanket on the floor.
2. Arrange for background music, preferably classical. You may have some aromatic incense burning. Dress in comfortable old clothes (a T-shirt and jeans, or pajamas). This exercise is best done at your regular mealtime so you will be hungry.
3. After your blindfold is in place, your partner will guide you to the center of the blanket, where you will sit cross-legged. The menu, prepared by your partner, should be unknown to you.
4. Once you are comfortably seated, your partner will bring in the food. You are not to use your own hands — you will be fed by your partner.
5. When the food is before you, try to guess what has been prepared, using your sense of smell. Sounds may give you a clue, too.
6. Your partner will proceed to feed you, using his or her fingers only — no utensils. Liquids may be ingested through a straw. This is an experience calling for the utmost in cooperation and intuitive awareness because you must also refrain from talking or making any extraneous movements with your hands.
7. Your partner has the responsibility of putting food into your mouth at an appropriate pace and in a bite size that is right for you. You will need to have implicit trust in your partner. In this exercise you will experience again, in a small way, the marvelous rapport between mother and child.

You will undoubtedly find that you are forced, during this exercise, to use your lips and tongue as primary touch sensors, and your tongue will dart out to clean not only your lips but even the fingers that feed you. How well you communicate with your partner will determine when you get the next bite or a drink.

Partners can switch roles for the next meal so that each can experience the sensation of feeding and being fed.

THE BLIND SHOWER

The next time you take a shower, turn the bathroom light off and close your eyes tightly or use a blindfold from the moment you step into the shower until you have dried yourself off. This is not as difficult as it seems, since you've undoubtedly taken the same shower countless times and know by habit where everything is. (Be sure to have a nonslip mat on the bottom of the shower stall — but you should have one there all the time, anyway.) You may finish the exercise with a new respect for how much you can do with your remaining senses and your intuition.

1. Feel the steam in your nose, note how different everything sounds when you splash in the dark.
2. Feel the water on your closed eyelids.
3. Find the soap (yes, you will know where it usually is). Soap yourself and note how different it feels when you don't see your body as you soap it. If you drop the soap, try to find it without opening your eyes. Your sense of hearing will tell you where it fell.
4. Don't open your eyes until you are out of the shower, dried yourself, and put on your bathrobe or clothes.

THE DUMB TV EXERCISE

Tune in to your favorite program on TV, *turn the sound off,* and try to follow the action and plot line. At first it may seem that being deaf would be a terrible handicap. But after a while you will find yourself sensing nonaudible clues and you may be surprised to find that you can piece together the story from the soundless screen by reading the lips, gestures, body language, and movements of the actors.

It is well known that our visual observation is far greater than our conscious is aware of. Recently, for example, police investigators in Ukiah, California, were able to obtain a description of a kidnapper from five-year-old Timmy White by hypnotizing the child. Under hypnosis, Timmy recalled vivid details of his abductor's appearance that he was not able to describe otherwise. Hypnosis, which is treated in detail in another chapter, helps put the conscious into a recessive role and allows the intuitive to become dominant. Timmy's recall of his abductor's appearance is a dramatic example that visually we absorb more than we are conscious of.

At least one private detective in New York City, Andrea Forrest, routinely uses hypnosis to obtain from a victim a more accurate description of the assailant. This is not mere trickery, but a way to tap nonverbal knowledge, often acquired in an instant and retained in the right brain, as in the Quick Look Exercise below.

THE QUICK LOOK, OR TACHISTOSCOPE, EXERCISE

In this exercise, you can duplicate the effect of a tachisto-scope, a device used to speed up reading comprehension by exposing a visual stimulus for a fraction of a second. All you will need is a picture book.

1. Place the open picture book in front of you and close your eyes. Open your eyes for an instant, glimpse the picture in the book, and quickly close your eyes again.
2. Try to remember what you saw; fill in as much detail as possible. Open your eyes and look at the picture again.
3. How much did you remember?
4. Repeat this experiment with other pictures.

With practice, you will find that you are seeing more, faster, and remembering it more vividly. You will have learned to bypass the conscious and to rely more on the intuitive.

If you can obtain the use of a tachistoscope somewhere, it

can be helpful in coaxing your intuitive to help in both observing and remembering. The tachistoscope exposes either colors, figures, or other visual stimuli for an instant (the timing can be speeded up or slowed down). As you speed up the instrument's time, you will find yourself comprehending the exposed stimulus in a shorter and shorter period of time, yet your recall may be as good or even better at the faster speed. This is attributable to the sharpening and opening up of your intuitive comprehension.

THE OLFACTORY EXERCISE

Though civilization has made the sense of smell less crucial to man's survival, smell is still an important sense.

Despite all our bathing and deodorants we each give off an odor that is unique. Think of how the bloodhound performs. Once the dog has smelled an article of your clothing he can track you for minutes or days. Your invisible imprint is recorded in his nose.

Although this tracking ability may be attenuated in man, many of our intuitive clues come from our sense of smell, which, incidentally, has the most direct connection to our behavior centers and which, therefore, often totally bypasses the conscious. The real reason you are attracted or repelled by someone may be due to a scent signal of which you are totally unaware. Our olfactory sense has been measured to be 10,000 times more sensitive than our sense of taste. It gives us psychological, gustatory, and sexual pleasure, and perhaps much more than we know.

The exercise described below inhibits only a minute fraction of your smelling potential, but it does make the point. It will demonstrate how insipid your life would be without the sense of smell.

1. Place a bit of cotton in each nostril. Make sure it is large enough to effectively shut off your sense of smell and tight enough so that it doesn't fall out.
2. Now go about your normal breakfast routine. You will notice that food tastes flat. The orange juice is like dishwater. The coffee lacks zest. And you didn't notice that the toast was burning until it was too late. There will be many more effects, perhaps too subtle to articulate, but you will have a heightening feeling of anxiety until the cotton is removed.

FORCED DECISIONS

These next exercises are designed to force you to make immediate decisions, thereby bypassing the conscious and forcing the intuitive to act. They are excellent training for saving time in the future; we make countless conscious decisions each day that can be delegated to the intuitive.

THE TEN-SECOND DECISION EXERCISE

In this exercise you will make a series of decisions within ten seconds. To give you a better idea of how long ten seconds take you may start by setting a kitchen timer for ten seconds. Try to use this timer whenever appropriate.

1. Start the day by deciding in ten seconds what you are going to wear.
2. When you go to lunch, make your selection from the menu in ten seconds.
3. On your next trip to the supermarket, take the list of things you need, but take only ten seconds to select each item.
4. The next time you buy a necktie or scarf, force yourself to make the choice in ten seconds and then live with it.
5. Pack your bag for a trip taking only ten seconds to decide on

each item you will take. (You may be surprised to find out how well you do.)

6. In playing chess, checkers, or bridge, take only ten seconds to decide on your move or the card you will play.

7. If you had to leave your house because of fire, plan what would you take — in ten seconds.

All the experiences given above are designed to give you greater fluency with the language of your intuitive system. Add any decisions you like to this list. As your confidence grows, your decision-making process will be speeded up.

6

Biofeedback Breakthrough

Biofeedback is a revolutionary healing technique that enables you to influence and control your autonomic system. Although it is taught with the help of simple electronic or mechanical equipment, it can eventually be done using only your intuition and your powers of concentration. It has opened up an extraordinary world of self-help and is a way to learn what is happening inside your body beyond the level of your conscious control.

Every moment of your life you receive millions of signals, which call for some kind of body adjustment in order to adapt to the world around you. The healthy human body is a miracle of efficiency. You sneeze, your pupils dilate, you perspire, or your blood pressure goes up — all changes brought about *without your conscious control,* due to external changes of temperature, light, dust, danger, or internal self-monitoring systems. Doctors refer to this as the *autonomic nervous system* — meaning a system that is involuntary and "runs itself."

In brief, here is how the autonomic nervous system works.

When there is a change in the environment, your senses send signals to control centers in your body where they are integrated with information previously stored in your brain or nervous system. Without your knowing what is going on, new messages are sent out with directions for appropriate body reactions.

Many of the devices used to check our inner signals are familiar: the thermometer for body temperature, the blood pressure arm cuff, the stethoscope for listening to the heart, and the electrocardiogram for recording heart activity, to name but a few. Experiments, conducted to date with heartening success, demonstrate that a person can be trained to recognize internal signals and control the action of inner organs.

With biofeedback training, it is possible to monitor and evaluate internal signals that were previously inaccessible. Today, an individual can be trained to follow, on a conscious level, his brain waves, blood pressure, temperature, heartbeat, pulse, and muscle tension. Here's how it works:

A device picks up the internal signal you want to follow and records it by means of a light beam or a sound. The patient is able to note responses of his inner body through the changing light or tone on the monitoring device.

He tries to achieve a desired result by "willing" something to happen inside himself. When this is achieved, the monitor instantly records it, giving the patient confirmation of his success. He tries to repeat whatever he did until he learns to get the result he wants even without the aid of the monitor. This is a perfect example of the conscious and intuitive working together.

DANNY'S HEADACHE AND BIOFEEDBACK

My friend Danny M. had chronic migraine headaches. He tried everything possible to relieve the pain — drugs, massage, hypnosis, diversion, special diets, and meditation — but never had any significant results. Doctors suggested that the head-aches might subside if he could relax, and he himself noticed that whenever he was with certain friends he relaxed and the pain was eased.

Then Danny heard about biofeedback training and de-cided to give it a try. This is how he described his experience to me:

"During the training sessions, I would sit in a comfortable chair, get as relaxed as I could, strap a tension meter to my arm, and observe the activity of the needle on the meter.

"I would make a conscious effort to lower the reading on the meter. Sometimes my efforts backfired and the needle would go up instead of down, and I would try again to make some internal adjustment of my body tension to correct it.

"After many sessions I was able to create minute increases and decreases in muscle tension in my body, and I learned to control the needle merely by *willing* it. I was able to learn how to control muscle tension by an unconscious internal process, and eventually I learned to get relief from my headaches just by willing it."

Similar results have been achieved by others whose prob-lems involved blood pressure, an irregular heartbeat, elevated body temperatures, and other autonomically controlled body symptoms.

BIOFEEDBACK AND INTUITION

You are no doubt wondering what this has to do with intuition. Remember our definition of intuition: knowing something without being aware of how you know. The gap between the two systems has been bridged, *from the intuitive to the conscious.* In the biofeedback phenomenon we have the opposite: The gap is bridged *from the conscious to the intuitive.*

You consciously try to achieve a change inside your body: Your intuitive system attempts to comply. In an experiment, when it in fact does what is wanted, the conscious mind picks it up through the external device and, in doing so, encourages and reinforces the action of the intuitive.

Through biofeedback you can learn to control an internal process *without being aware of how you achieved the result.* In an experiment, when patients learned to control something as completely internal as blood pressure, *none of them were able to describe what they did to lower their blood pressure.*

YOU CAN USE BIOFEEDBACK TO ENCOURAGE INTUITION

Biofeedback techniques can be used to develop intuitive power. In fact, if you are still unconvinced about the scope of the intuitive system, I recommend that you arrange for a biofeedback demonstration at one of the many biofeedback laboratories that have sprung up all over the country. Almost every college has a department working on it, and they are usually happy to have new subjects to work with in their studies.

In your first session you will be instructed to look for a certain type of wave on the oscilloscope or a light that will appear when you achieve the internal condition you are seeking. At first you will hit it only by accident; you will be told to try to do whatever you did internally to make it happen again.

After a while you may be able to repeat whatever you did to get the results you want internally — despite the fact that you will remain totally unaware of *how* you did it.

We do not know how intuitive awareness comes about; neither do we know how the individual is able to control what was originally an unconscious process.

Success with biofeedback will surely be an inspiration, for it will prove to you that *results can be achieved without awareness of how they are achieved* — just as in intuition.

The great advantage of the biofeedback monitoring device is the instant dramatic confirmation of the result achieved. With intuition we rarely have such immediate and certain confirmation. We only have an internal feeling that the intuitive revelation is correct; we must wait for the future to provide an opportunity to prove it right or wrong.

However, just as you can learn to get biofeedback results without the meter, light, or tone signal, you can learn to trust your intuition without need for immediate confirmation.

7

Solving Problems
the Creative Way

Language can become a screen which stands between the
thinker and reality. This is the reason that true creativity often
starts where language ends.
— Arthur Koestler, in *The Act of Creation*

A problem is any perplexing situation to which you must react
to achieve a goal. Ordinary living involves a constant process of
problem solution. Indeed, solving problems is the crux, the
very essence, of the life experience. Do not say that you want to
get rid of the problems in your life, because if you do, you are
saying that you do not want a life of growth and change and
challenge.

How you solve your particular problems determines, in
many ways, the quality of your life. Learning to solve them
creatively can help make your life more exciting and reward-
ing.

People who consistently come up with exciting solutions
and ways to do things are described as "creative." All of us start

life with a great creative potential; some develop this creative ability, while others, alas, permit it to lie dormant or to atrophy.

In my classes on Applied Creativity I often use a kaleidoscope to demonstrate how the mind creates new ideas or solutions. The kaleidoscope is a hollow tube with bits and pieces of colored stones and glass with several mirrors at one end. Holding the opposite end up to your eye, you can turn the tube and watch the pieces tumble — and as they tumble, they form new groupings, picked up by the mirrors to form endless new patterns. In a similar way, your mind takes bits and pieces of information and experience, tumbles them about, and produces new ideas.

These are the steps by which most people deal with a problem:

1. You become aware of the problem.
2. You study it to explore all of its aspects.
3. You try to recall solutions that worked in the past for a similar problem.
4. You may use logic and reasoning to follow through the consequences of any steps you consider.
5. You may use your imagination to visualize a new, untried solution, and you mentally test it by imagining the results and side effects of this solution. (This step may utilize unusual combinations of information stored in your memory bank, both conscious and intuitive.)
6. If you find no solution that seems satisfactory, you may repeat all of the steps or give up for a while — or even for good.

Many solutions are found through the steps outlined above, but often there is another part to the problem-solving process: *incubation.*

INCUBATION

Incubation is a pause in the process of problem solving, a mysterious period when conscious thinking about the problem is dormant and the intuitive voice has a chance to break through.

During this time, the intuitive system searches and assembles bits of its stored information that might be relevant to the problem and tries to bring these to the attention of the conscious. The "spark," or sudden bridging of the gap when intuitive information is added to what you have developed by logic, illuminates and reveals the solution you have been seeking.

An idea may be the product of an incubation period that started days, months, or even years earlier. You may have grappled with a problem for days with no apparent solution. You forget it for a while — to all outward appearances, you have given up trying to solve the problem — and you move on to other things. Then suddenly, seemingly out of nowhere, an idea springs into your mind spontaneously, with the long-sought-for solution. How did this happen?

The intuitive mind retained the problem on an unconscious level — "on a back burner" — and in time it broke through and contributed stored intuitive knowledge to the solution. Incubation enabled you to make connections between present knowledge and stored unconscious information. It is the processing phase of the intuitive system, and it can take a few seconds — or years.

Ampere, for whom the amp is named, detailed in his diary his first discovery thus: "On April 27, I gave a shout of joy . . . *seven years ago* I proposed to myself a problem which I have not been able to solve. At last, *I do not know how,* I found it . . ." [the solution]. [Emphasis mine.]
— Dr. J. C. Gowan, *Journal of Applied Creativity* (spring 1979)

Julia Child, otherwise known as the French Chef of TV fame, and a brilliant woman with many talents besides gourmet cooking, wrote this to me in a recent letter:

> . . . You have considerable baggage in the back of your mind . . . and when you try out some new way of solving a problem and it is unsuccessful, other approaches well up from your subconscious.

The same thing was said another way by Pasteur when he noted that "inspiration — (i.e., the great idea) — is the impact of a newly observed fact on a mind that has been fully prepared for it by prior absorption of knowledge."

And the lovable folk philosopher, humorist, and author, Sam Levenson, gave me his theory:

> A concept *ostensibly* arrived at rationally (I've experienced it while writing a book or addressing an audience) is taken over by a nonrational feeling. Tugging my mind toward some truth which I was not aware of, it proceeds to speak to me, sometimes for me. I suddenly become conscious of knowing again what to the best of my knowledge I never knew before. Call it awakening, perhaps reawakening, of a knowingness which reveals itself to me of its own will, not mine. Call it a higher intelligence from some lower depth which dictates the words this revelation requires. These "gut" stirrings then become information — perhaps some stored-away information which has been alive and available but unrecognized by me until it decided to come to my aid by adding to reason what reason itself could not deliver.
>
> I am always awestruck when this happens, no matter how often it happens. I've learned by now to wait for it.

SOLVING PROBLEMS CREATIVELY

Enormously creative people have the ability to (1) go through the usual problem-solving steps very rapidly, (2) cut the incubation period, in some cases to as little as a few seconds, (3) welcome the input of the intuitive, and (4) suspend judgmental faculties for a while in order to give full consideration to every bit of information from the intuitive.

It was while teaching my classes in Applied Creativity over the years that I became increasingly aware of the symbiosis of creativity and intuition. What, indeed, causes the inspired perception, the "Aha!" response, and the spark of — for lack of a better word — *genius,* in some people, while others, just as intelligent, plod along mired down with day-to-day details, with never a new idea or an inspired vision?

Creative people, I discovered, are extraordinarily intuitive, and intuitive people are usually creative; the two qualities seem to be inextricably intertwined. Creative people seem to have an innate and apparently untutored ability to put aside their judgmental or self-critical faculty when their intuition bombards them with ideas.

This ability has been noticed by others. As far back as 1788, the poet and philosopher Friedrich Schiller wrote to a friend suffering from a creative block:

> It seems a bad thing and detrimental to the creative work of the mind if Reason makes too close an examination of ideas as they come pouring in. . . .
>
> Where there is a creative mind, Reason — so it seems to me — relaxes its watch upon the gates, and the ideas rush in pell-mell, and only then does it look them through and examine them. . . .
>
> You . . . are ashamed or frightened of the momentary and transient extravagances which are to be found in all truly creative minds and whose longer or shorter duration distinguish the thinking artist from the dreamer. You complain of your unfruitfulness *because you reject too soon and discriminate too severely.* [Emphasis mine.]

And Freud advocated "the adoption of an attitude of uncritical self-observation" in order to increase input from what he termed the "unconscious mind" — what we today know is the intuitive right side of the brain. In his writings on creativity, he said:

> We are probably inclined to overestimate the conscious character of intellectual and artistic production. . . . Accounts given us by some of the most highly productive men, such as Goethe and Helmholtz, show rather that what is essential and new in their creations came to them without premeditation and as an almost ready-made whole.

OPENING UP TO CREATIVITY

Why does the artist have the ability to generate creative solutions to problems? It may be due to having a parent who encouraged ideas; or the influence of a teacher at a crucial time in his development. It may be the cumulative effect of an environment. For example, a young girl whose childhood had been exceptionally deprived developed an unusual genius with words because she had no toys and nothing to do but read the books she was able to get free at the public library.

We have no definitive knowledge about what produces a creative genius. It seems relatively easy to create a well-behaved child, a studious child, and even a child who is a model good citizen; but no one has yet been able to identify the life differentials that produced a Tolstoy, a Beethoven, an Einstein, a Madame Curie, a Chaplin, or a Picasso.

The truth is, we open ourselves up to creativity in the same way we open ourselves up to intuition. *The more facile your intuition, the more rapidly you move from incubation to creative problem solution.* In other words, as you develop greater and faster input from your intuition, you reach creative solutions faster and better.

When do you get your best ideas? For each of us, there are certain times when ideas germinate more readily — when the "great" solution is more likely to materialize. Over the years I've asked each class the above question. The answers range widely, from "just before falling asleep" to "while shaving in the morning" and "while driving to Hartford." However individual, in every case the left brain has been given a rest, and intuition from the right brain has had a chance to leap across the gap.

When I'm faced with a very difficult decision or the need to find a truly creative solution, I take a nice hot shower. I have a wooden stool in the shower stall. I make myself comfortable and let the warm water cascade on my head and body. Sooner or later the idea blooms. I repeat the idea to myself, aloud, several times, to make sure I won't forget it, before I turn the water to cold.

Since we're each unique, study yourself to find out when you achieve your best ideas and don't hesitate to exploit this special insight.

THE INTUITIVE DIARY

The Intuitive Diary will give you another way to observe, monitor, and verify the validity of your intuitive insights. It will encourage you to invoke your intuition in solving your problems creatively — and it will also help to speed up the incubation period.

After you have used the diary for a period of time, you may want to look back to see how your intuitive power has developed, how clearly you are now able to dissect your problems, and how quickly you can call on your nonverbal system to aid in the solution of any problem.

Here are the steps for starting an Intuitive Diary:

1. Get a hard-cover bound book with blank pages, available at any bookstore. They are available with locks to assure you of privacy, if that will make you more comfortable.

2. Divide each page into three columns. These represent three phases of a learning process. In column one you will focus on something that is a problem to you. Here you will have an opportunity to set it all out exactly as it happened, with no emotion, judgments, or reaction — just the facts. In column two, the intuitive is invited to have its say. And in column three, you will discover you have reached a new understanding of the problem with input from both sides of the brain.

Let's explore these three phases in more detail.

3. Column one will become a record of all pertinent original data. You may be familiar with ordinary diaries, the kind that record the day-to-day activities of the diarist in some detail. They have a tendency to get boring, and keeping a diary like this for very long is difficult for most people. Not so with the Intuitive Diary. You record *only* the factual circumstances of the problem that is troubling you at the moment, whether it concerns career, health, sex, marriage, children, or any other matter. Do not record the trivia of the day. Write as objectively as you can. Tell what happened to cause your problem — externally and inside you. Each entry should be dated. Here is an example.

Monday, November 1. Mr. Martin, my boss, stormed into the office and glared at all the girls in my department. He started to yell about the fact that someone had left the door to the building unlocked on Friday night, that all the records and merchandise could have been stolen. He went on repeating, Who could have done it? Even though it was in front of all my staff, I blurted out that I was the last one to leave on Friday and I might have done it, but it would never happen again. Mr. Martin seemed almost upset by my confessing, but only said, "OK" as he left the room. I felt terrible; my hands were trembling and my heart was pounding.

The pertinent data of column one are not limited to events or incidents: They can reflect any experience that concerns you — dreams, emotions, feelings — but they should be evidence of first impression.

4. Before you write in column two, perform one of the exercises to quiet your left brain: close your eyes, get comfortable, breathe deeply for relaxation, and empty your mind of all directed thought as you summon your intuitive. Now go over the details you have written in column one. Visualize the whole scene again and, as it unfolds, allow your attention to wander. Permit other details to surface. Accept awarenesses that you missed before. Drop any judgmental barriers. Record these new insights as faithfully as possible in the order in which they occurred to you in column two. Column two may now contain new facts, images, symbols, or even little vignettes that on the surface seem unrelated to the problem at hand.

5. Column three will be filled in later — a few hours later, or perhaps days, or even weeks later. Column three will record the outcome of the intutitive message in column two as applied to the facts in column one. You will recognize the "Aha!" effect, the clicking into place.

Each of us has his own individual way of learning. The phases represented by columns one, two, and three may not unfold neatly or within a given period of time. Perhaps you will fill in column two later — hours or days later — after filling in column one. Find out what is best for you. Be guided by your own insights as they occur.

Here is the example we started above from Alice R.'s Intuitive Diary. She is thirty-one, single, and helps support her parents.

COLUMN ONE	COLUMN TWO	COLUMN
Monday,	*Tuesday,*	THREE
November 1.	*November 2.*	*May 3.*
Facts of confron-	Mr. Martin was	I became con-
tation: Mr. Mar-	angry all right	vinced that Mr.

COLUMN ONE
(cont.)

tin, my boss, stormed into the office and glared at all the girls in my department. He started to yell about the fact that someone had left the door to the building open on Friday night, that all the records and merchandise could have been stolen. He went on repeating, who could have done it? Even though it was in front of all my staff, I blurted out that I was the last to leave on Friday and I might have done it, but it would never happen again. Mr. Martin seemed almost upset by my confessing, but only said "OK" as he

COLUMN TWO
(cont.)

— but there was something forced about it. When he looked around the room at everybody he looked twice at me. . . . Now I remember that Helen, my assistant, had a sort of smile as Mr. Martin was yelling. Then I saw a tree with a vine wrapped around it. When I decided to tell the truth and spoke up, Mr. Martin seemed disappointed. Why? He knew it was me all the time. He wanted to trap me! Why? Helen, of course — they're friends — Mr. Martin would like to fire me after all, and then give my job to Helen, the

COLUMN THREE
(cont.)

Martin wanted to get rid of me, and so I started to look for another job. I found a perfect one but I was worried about giving Mr. Martin as my reference. I hadn't really been so good, but he gave me a great reference and 1 got the job! Helen was immediately appointed to my old job. When I said good-bye to them, we parted on friendly terms, but I could see they were both relieved.

COLUMN ONE (cont.)	COLUMN TWO (cont.)	COLUMN THREE (cont.)
left the room. I felt terrible; my hands were trembling and my heart was pounding.	clinging vine.	

Alice was very upset by the incident when it happened, but she couldn't figure out 'why. Nothing earthshaking had happened. She hadn't been fired or even reprimanded when she admitted being the "culprit." Then why was she so disturbed? Information in column two, from her intuitive system, helped make it all clear: The boss was looking for a reason to fire her. If she had kept quiet and tried to hide the fact that it was she who had left the door unlocked, that would have given him enough reason to fire her.

She also intuited *why* he wanted to get rid of her: It was obvious that he was developing an attachment to Helen and wanted to promote her.

The arrival of this timely insight was vitally important to Alice. It gave her a chance to succeed in a situation in which she had been headed for disaster. The boss was given a chance to act like a nice guy, and everyone more or less got what he or she wanted. But without the intuitive input, it is likely that Alice would have been fired eventually.

Here is another example. Steven S. is a successful attorney, married, with two grown children. His entry in column one records a dream he couldn't forget after awakening.

COLUMN ONE	COLUMN TWO	COLUMN THREE
Thursday, July 5.	*Friday, July 6.*	*Monday, July 9.*
Last night I had	Once I felt totally	

COLUMN ONE
(cont.)

a very unusual
dream, not be-
cause it was wild
or fantastic, but
because I found it
very amusing as I
dreamed and very
depressing when
I woke. Here's
what I remember:
I was buying some
Bartel Bonds, 6
1/2 of 1988, con-
vertibles, to give
to my wife as an
anniversary gift.
Every time I tried
to complete the
purchase an old
pair of army boots
would crowd out
the scene. I would
try to clean the
boots. They
looked fine on top
but very muddy in
the cracks be-
tween the soles
and the upper
leather. I kept try-
ing to brush the
mud out with a

COLUMN TWO
(cont.)

relaxed I started
to go over the
dream very care-
fully. I kept asking
why as it un-
folded. Why was
I buying bonds?
What anniver-
sary? Why the
boots? Why
couldn't I get
them clean? Sud-
denly I knew;
They couldn't be
cleaned. They
were inherently
dirty! Why did
they crowd out
the bond buying?
"Aha!" — the
bonds were
dirty — there was
something inher-
ently wrong with
them. Now why
was I buying
bonds for my
wife's anniver-
sary? Ah, I was
negotiating to
make a loan for
her to one of my

COLUMN THREE
(cont.)

I called my client
and told him that
my wife had
changed her mind
about the mort-
gage. I went back
and reviewed all
the financial data
he had given me
about the busi-
ness and was as-
tonished to find
out it had been
getting progres-
sively worse dur-
ing the past four
years! I had al-
ways thought of
him as a very suc-
cessful busi-
nessman. The
business was re-
ally sick.

COLUMN ONE
(cont.)

toothbrush, but
no luck — the
mud stuck. Since
this was a "lucid
dream" I directed
the action back to
the bonds because
I thought they
were a very good
buy, but the
muddy boots kept
coming back. I
laughed when I
awoke but soon
began to feel de-
pressed.

COLUMN TWO
(cont.)

clients who of-
ferred to give a
mortage on the
business building
as security. He
also offered to
give her the op-
tion of converting
the mortgage into
equity in the bus-
iness. That was it!
My intuition was
warning me
against the
deal — there's
something wrong
with the business.
I feel good about
the whole phase
two process.

COLUMN
THREE
(cont.)

Stephen S. had permitted a past business relationship to blind him to the changes that had occurred in his client's business. But his intuition saw the whole picture and brought it to his attention.

Lori G. is twenty-two, intelligent, high-strung, and single.

COLUMN ONE
Sunday, May 3.
The party was
great. I met

COLUMN TWO
Monday, May 11.
He never called. I
kept wondering

COLUMN
THREE
Sunday, May 17.
After phase two, I

COLUMN ONE
(cont.)

Johnny, a super
guy. He's tall and
kind of wiry — fun
to dance with. I.
spent most of the
time with him.
We talked up a
storm. He's an
only child, his
parents are sepa-
rated. He works
in a bank and likes
to write poetry. I
felt so good and
I'm sure he likes
me and he'll take
me out soon.

COLUMN TWO
(cont.)

why, and finally
tried phase two.
When I reached
the twilight zone
I went over the
whole evening —
the fun of talking
and dancing to-
gether, the fact
that we liked the
same foods and
movies and cars.
It was all so great,
even when he
took me home.
He started to
reach out to kiss
me and I automat-
ically pulled back
just a little, and
like a gentleman
he stopped . . .
sort of laughed;
and later when he
said good-night,
he added, "I'll be
seeing you." At
this point, my old
dog, "Snuggles,"
floated into the
picture. I re-
member when my

COLUMN
THREE
(cont.)

knew why Johnny
hadn't called and
so I called him. As
soon as he an-
swered the
phone, I knew I
was right. He was
so glad to hear
from me. I said I
had a question
about banking to
ask him, but he
just sort of passed
over it and asked
me what I was
doing Saturday
night. We went to
a dance recital. It
was great, and so
was Johnny.

COLUMN ONE (cont.)	COLUMN TWO (cont.)	COLUMN THREE (cont.)
	father put the puppy down in front of me for the first time I reached out to pat him and he cringed and drew back. I cried and said over and over, "He doesn't like me." It was only later when my father urged me to try again that Snuggles and I became friends and inseparable. Johnny thought I didn't like him. He was shy — I noticed that at the beginning of the party.	

Lori thought she was being friendly the first evening. She had tried to encourage a relationship — but she forgot that actions often speak louder than words. Her intuition, however, had taken it all in, and when it made her aware of the problem, she was able to correct it.

8

Decision Making

I consider my intuition to be a key element of the mental processes that lead me to conclusions and to decisions.

— Henry Ford II
Chairman of the Board of Directors,
Ford Motor Company

People who find decisions hard to make are usually victims of the Delayed Decision, the Non-Decision, or the Wrong Decision syndromes — all mechanisms we resort to in fear of making a mistake. In a circuitous fashion, this fear becomes a self-fulfilling prophecy.

Let's examine each one of these mistakes in decision making.

THE DELAYED DECISION

The person who puts off a decision does so because it is too difficult or distasteful, and he hopes something will happen so that he won't have to make it. There are times when this is a perfectly proper strategy: when you need time to get more information to do the job right, or when a delay will change the circumstances in your favor.

Some people, however, make the Delayed Decision their *modus operandi:* They are ever fearful they may make a mistake, and they freeze, like an animal that is caught in the headlights of an approaching car on a highway and becomes unable to move.

The confused psychodynamics that go on in the head of the decision delayer are, "If I procrastinate, maybe I won't have to make the decision, or someone will come along and make it for me, and I won't be responsible if it turns out badly."

Delaying may indeed force someone else to make the decision, but not necessarily in your best interests. And delaying may ultimately eliminate the need for making *any* decision — but an opportunity may be lost.

THE NON-DECISION

The non-decider has no intention of ever reaching a decision. This method of coping has its roots in the same fears and uncertainties that assail the decision delayer, but the non-decider won't even bother to agonize about the choices, he simply allows circumstances or other people to make decisions for him. The non-decider hopes that if the decision turns out to be a bad one, he can say, *"It's not my fault, I wouldn't have chosen that option."* But if it turns out well, he can take the credit for his wisdom.

Besides, making our own decisions allows us to direct our own lives. When you leave your decisions to someone else, you deny yourself the opportunity to be a self-directed creative adult in charge of your own destiny.

THE WRONG DECISION

There are certain people whose whole lives are a series of bad decisions; they seem to be locked into a bad-decision syndrome. Happily there is a way of breaking this cycle: Bring your intuitive into the decision-making process!

YOU NEVER GET ALL THE FACTS

It is obvious that you can make a better decision when you have all the facts. Every time a new fact is added to the scales, it tips the balance to one side or the other. When you get enough facts, eventually one side emerges as the clear choice.

But when do you have all the facts? This is the question that bedevils all of us.

Success favors the chance-taker. If you wait until every conceivable fact is in, you may never make the decision, the opportunity may pass, or the decision may be made for you by someone else.

Indeed, weighing all the facts before making a decision is correct only in theory. In practice, we always make decisions on fewer than all the facts *because we can never get all the facts.*

The guide we must use is the same as the legal principle applied in civil cases: "the preponderance of the evidence." People who have trouble making decisions keep looking for more and more evidence. They look for a course of action that is right "beyond a reasonable doubt," the rule applied in criminal cases.

Let the intuitive guide you to quick, right decisions. Remember, the intuitive system has been gathering and storing information about your problem as long as you have been considering it. This holistic, nonverbal intelligence will factor in the long view, the overview, and the relevance of everything else that is important in your life. It does not let the mundane details of everyday life obscure its vision.

LOUDER THAN WORDS

For the past five years Arlene forged ahead in the man's world of investment banking. She became a senior analyst for a large firm. Her job was to invest the surplus capital in new ventures. Although quite successful, Arlene began to feel that there was no real future for her. Despite her department's great record, nobody seemed to care. She scouted for a new job and in a short time got a wonderful offer. When she gave notice to the president, however, he was appalled. Twenty-four hours later he offered her an excellent contract with an increase in salary plus the title of vice-president. There was also a hint that she might hope to have his job someday.

Arlene was very impressed and said she'd think it over. At home, in review, it all looked so great, but her intuition kept nagging her, and although she should have been elated with the turn of events, she felt depressed. She kept struggling with her decision, turning every facet over in her mind. But whenever she leaned toward staying she felt bad. Finally she decided she would take the new job. She immediately felt great.

Three months later Arlene learned that her former company had been sold to a corporate giant in the Midwest, and the employees were given a choice of moving or resigning. Although all the negotiations had been in the deepest secret, Arlene's intuition had guided her correctly. Her boss was desperately trying to keep her while he was negotiating the sale.

SHELLEY'S FRIEND

A friend of my daughter's, a woman who is a successful clinical psychologist, is kind enough to share this experience:
"Once intuition saved my whole career. I was in grad-

uate school, an honor student, and lucky enough to have two outstanding professors in the psychology department vying to have me work toward my doctorate under them. It was a difficult decision to make: One was very famous and an influential man at the university; the other was highly respected, but since he did not have tenure there was a possibility that he might transfer to another university before I completed the courses for my degree — which would leave me without continuity in my graduate program. I was sought out and interviewed by both professors; they each seemed to want me as a protégée.

"One day, the famous one, whom I'll call Dr. X, invited me to lunch. We went to a Chinese restaurant, and as we ate, I was a bit startled when Dr. X leaned over and started to eat from my dish. I don't mind sharing, and I like to taste new dishes that my friends order at Chinese restaurants, but he didn't even ask or comment, he just reached across the table, took a forkful, ate it, then took another, and said, 'You need more soy sauce.' I started to taste my food and he said, 'Take my word for it. It needs more soy sauce.'

"We finished lunch. I was dazzled by his brilliance, and it seemed he was the logical choice for me. It was only in the stillness of the night, in my bed, that I began to have some misgivings, and as I let my feelings go, I became aware that somehow he would be the wrong choice for me.

"I chose the other professor, even though there was a risk that he might leave. As a matter of fact, he *did* leave two years later, but I was so far along in my graduate program that I was able to finish my thesis and get my degree on time anyway.

"It's ironic, but *not one* of my friends who decided to work with the famous Dr. X ever got a doctorate.

"My intuition told me to stay away from him despite his brilliance because he would be too dominating and possessive. As I tell you the story now, you can see the clue on which the intuitive decision was made because I have pointed it up. But I assure you that I was completely unconscious of it at the time. It made no impression on my conscious mind: We had spent over two hours at that lunch, and I had been aflame with the ideas we discussed and the glamour of being his disciple. You can see now why I trust my intuition."

MAKING A DECISION ABOUT YOUR FUTURE

From Washington, D.C., columnist Art Buchwald, witty observer of the capital scene, wrote to describe how he made certain career decisions in his life:

> Intuition has always played a part in my life. In 1948, something told me to go to Paris. I went and stayed fourteen years and started my newspaper career there. In 1962, intuition told me to move to Washington. It was the best move I could have made at the time . . . I don't know what intuition is, but I guess it's a feeling that one should do something at a particular time.

If you are at a point in your life when you have an important decision to make about your future career, or when you don't know what kind of work you might be suited for, or where or how you would like to live, you can call upon your intuition to help guide you. The exercise below can be a valuable tool in pinpointing your life goals and helping you decide what course to take.

THE SCENARIO OF THE FUTURE

1. First, calm the left brain by going through the Basic Warm-up exercise.
2. When you are totally relaxed, with your eyes closed, visualize yourself in the role you want to try out. (The more you know about the role, the greater the validity of this exercise: some

homework beforehand may be called for.) Let us assume you are considering medicine as a career possibility: Visualize a day in a doctor's life with you in the starring role. Proceed through the doctor's day, filling in as much detail as you can. Watch yourself making your morning hospital rounds, scrubbing up for a routine tonsillectomy, seeing patients in your office, using a blood pressure cuff on an old man, looking down a child's throat, being called out in the middle of the night to tend to an emergency. Don't neglect visualizing yourself sending out the bills (or directing your office nurse to), reading stacks of medical journals, keeping medical charts — the mundane activities as well as the dramatic.

3. Throughout this scenario with you in the starring role, pay close attention to how you feel. Note any surges of joy, exhilaration, any deep satisfaction, and any distastefulness or vague disinterest. The more detailed a script you can imagine, the less likely you are to delude yourself.

4. When you emerge from this reverie, reflect on how you felt about the whole experience. Did you feel a tug at your heartstrings when you as the doctor examined the child's throat? Or boredom? Did you rush through it, or did you think of new ways to create an efficient, pleasant office? Did you feel comfortable in the role, or were you detached, observing a TV segment of "Dr. Kildare?"

5. You may want to make comparisons with other roles. Repeat the same process for a day in the life of an artist, housewife, interior decorator, engineer, or whomsoever you please. When you have done the exercise several times and made some intuitive comparisons, you will gradually become aware of which career you most enjoy on a realistic day-to-day level.

This exercise can be used for almost any kind of decision about your future. It helps you anticipate problems and eliminate the possibility of wasting time working toward a career you don't really want. It is sad to think of people spending years studying to become a doctor or engineer, only to find out that they don't like the actual day-to-day work and, more often than not, are not very good at it.

Still, our lives do not move in straight lines. There may be many times when you will have to reevaluate your life and chart a new course, whether you are twenty-five or fifty. Your intuition is your ever-faithful and reliable guide.

9

The Karma Connection and Other Strategies

Each year, in teaching the course in creativity, I help my students discover more about their true selves with the aid of an exercise I call the Karma Connection.

In early November I stroll on the lonely and abandoned beaches in my area. With a large brown bag in hand I amble along the beach and pick up bits of the flotsam and jetsam that wash up on deserted beaches: unusual shells, driftwood, feathers, pieces of rope, bits of charcoal, rocks, twigs, and crabshells. I put them in the brown bag, which I bring to class.

The students are instructed to reach into the brown bag, eyes closed, and pull out the first object they feel drawn to. It should not be a conscious or logical selection, but rather an impulse. Whatever they select becomes theirs alone, the item with which they will experience the Karma Connection.

You can find your own object during a walk in an area near you: a beach, a park, or some other place where you are likely to find natural or discarded objets d'art. Pick up something you seem drawn to. It can be anything. Don't look for it, don't plan it, don't evaluate it. Your choice should be an impulsive one.

After you have selected an object, your goal is to *find relevance between the object you picked and your life.*

1. Select a place where you can be alone and undisturbed for at least half an hour. Find a comfortable way to sit and place your talismanic object in front of you so that you can study it. The light should not be too bright, but bright enough so that you can carefully examine the object.

2. Turn the object over carefully in your hands, examine it from every angle.

3. Now place it about an arm's length away. With your eyes open, start the breathing exercise to relax, let all extraneous thoughts slip away, and focus on your talisman until there is nothing but you and it. As this concentration grows, you may experience a sense of merging with the object, a feeling of oneness between you and your talisman. You may become aware of a sense of knowing what it's all about, an understanding of God and the universe. This is the kind of experience that mystics, gurus, and spiritual leaders work so hard to achieve.

4. Do not give up in despair if you do not achieve this state. Not many people do. There is still much for you to learn from this experience. Look for the relevance between your talisman and your life.

One student, an engineer, produced an entire graph of his life from a piece of driftwood: The cracks and breaks in the wood seemed to reflect exactly the major changes in his life. A widow found the story of her life in a rock: The different colors and textures reflected her three children and her different relationships with them, and even the untimely death of her husband. She was convinced her talisman was mystical.

5. As you concentrate on the connection between you and the talisman, close your eyes, visualize the object, and allow the free-association process to work. Without directing your thoughts, note the images and fantasies and feelings that emerge.

6. When you have finished this phase of the exercise, stop, take a more comfortable position (you may lie down), close your eyes, and then, keeping in mind the relevance of the object to your life, review it for any insights, awareness, or new knowledge about your life and your inner self.

Some students have said that the talisman acted as a focal point on which to concentrate their thoughts. Others have reported that the experience revealed truths about themselves that ordinary unfocused contemplation never uncovered. Many were convinced that their destiny, or Karma, was reflected in that remote object in a mirrorlike way.

What has been most interesting in the years that students have been reporting on this experience is that with this exercise more than any other, they have been able to get in touch with their inner selves, the true essence of their Karma, destiny, or, for lack of a better word, soul.

Here are some additional strategies that may work for you. What enticement your intuitive will react to is sui generis to you alone. All of the exercises try to accomplish the same thing, but just as all food has a common function there is a world of difference in what suits your taste.

DANCING

In the privacy of your room — away from the sight and hearing of anyone — arrange for music of many different modes. As you play each selection allow yourself to move with the music. The movement may begin with nothing more than the swaying of your head or the tapping of a finger. As you let yourself go, however, involve more of your body and dance. Don't think — just listen and let your body react. When the music stops you may find your body wants to continue — let it. When you are through, lie on the floor or bed for a moment, close your eyes, do the Basic Warm-up, and note the feelings and thoughts that move through your mind.

Later you may want to explore what they mean to you. Use the Intuitive Key — ask "Why?"

This exercise should be repeated with different kinds of music until you find what music releases your intuitive. When you know, use it from time to time to start the process.

KNEADING

Evelyn Virshup, in her exciting book *Right Brain People in a Left Brain World,* prescribes an exercise she uses in Art Therapy that you can adopt for your own use.

Use clay or any material like clay, i.e. dough or putty, to create nondirective art. The kneading process itself, as you squeeze, mold, pound, or caress, will encourage some nonverbal understanding. Do it with your eyes closed — in silence — imagine the clay is you or a part of you. Start the Basic Warm-up, and as you work the clay, note what passes through your mind. Feel the changing forms you create: There may be metaphoric messages in the forms themselves or in the way you make them.

INK BLOT

Ms. Virshup also notes "that every mark we make on paper, all the colors and graphic gestures and forms we create are extensions of ourselves."

Try the following exercise to see what feedback it brings to you.

1. Take a sheet of white drawing paper.
2. Make a blot or two of ink or paint somewhere in the center.

3. Now fold the paper and press the part over the blot to spread it out in as bizarre a shape as you can.
4. Unfold the paper. Look at the blot. It will be similar to the forms used in a Rorschach test.
5. Turn the paper from side to side. What do you see? Is there something that is recognizable? Something that you would like to develop?
6. Now take paints or crayons and fill in with color what you see in the guidelines of the blots.
7. Look at what you've created. Imagine that you are what is on the paper. How does this make you feel?
8. Now close your eyes. Do the Basic Warm-up and explore the "why" of your creation and your response.

MUSICAL DOODLING

This is something you can do whether you're a musician or not. It has echoes of the Resonance effect, but is not so directed or structured. It is in fact a form of musical doodling.

Take a drum or pot or large bottle, anything that makes a sound when you tap or strike it. You can even use a musical instrument, a piano, guitar, saxophone, or whatever. Close your eyes. Now, instead of trying to play a melody or rhythm you recall, just make sounds — nondirected sounds; follow the sounds wherever they lead, randomly. As you doodle with sound, note how you feel and what goes through your mind.

After a while, stop. Close your eyes, do the Basic Warm-up, and recall what you've noted and wonder what it means.

Part II

APPLICATION

Thus far we have learned what intuition is, how it works, and how to use it. There have been exercises and strategies to help you experience intuitions. That is what an intuition is — an experience. As such, it is unique and meaningful to each of us. Your intuitive system furnishes you with signals just as the five senses do, and you must learn to interpret them just as you have learned to interpret what you see, hear, smell, taste, and feel. Doing so will allow you to apply intuition to your daily life.

In the last analysis you must always do this alone. The clues, guidelines, and insights in this book can only be effective when they are applied by you and used to work out the problems of your own life.

The following chapters are devoted to major aspects of life. The observations, anecdotes, and examples have been selected to enable you to profit intuitively as well as rationally.

10

Making a Living

So many of the problems we face arise from making a living. When you learn to tap your intuitive resources you're much more able to solve them. There may be little hard concrete evidence to point the right way, but some vision or feeling usually gives a clue to the intuitive solution. You can develop this characteristic by making a conscious effort to get intuitive input when you face a problem. Practice not only makes perfect, but more important, *practice makes facile.* As you succeed, problem solving the intuitive way becomes easier and easier, until eventually it becomes automatic.

Many of the world's most successful people freely acknowledge the use of intuition in their careers. In an article entitled "Those Business Hunches Are More than Blind Faith" in the April 23, 1979, issue of *Fortune* magazine, a sample of the country's leading businessmen credited intuition as a factor in their business decisions. John Fetzer, owner of the Detroit Tigers and chairman of Fetzer Broadcasting Company, said:

"Intuition helps you read between the lines: walk through an office — intuition tells you if things are going well."

And Alan Ladd, Jr., who has proved himself a genius in producing films that are big box-office successes, recently told the *Wall Street Journal:* "I realize this job can't last forever; my gut instinct for picking the right pictures might run out."

He was being modest; your intuition doesn't fail you any sooner than your thinking apparatus.

The insightful letter earlier quoted from Henry Ford II throws a new light on an aspect of intuition, discussed ironically enough by Alfred Sloan, Chairman of the Board of Directors of General Motors more than two generations ago. Sloan is reputed to have said that when all the facts, studies, and reports were in, *the final decision is often intuitive.* Ford's new contribution is reflected in the following:

> Intuitive reactions, I find, are usually valuable even if they prove to be wrong. *They give me an instant basis with which to compare alternatives* that may later be developed in the more usual ways of corporate practice. And when my intuition's right in the first instance, I am that far ahead at the outset. [Emphasis mine.]

In other words, your intuition can give you a yardstick against which to measure other ideas and also to guide you in making the final decision.

And here is an excerpt from a letter written to me by that multi-talented lady — author, television personality, and editor of *Cosmopolitan* magazine — Helen Gurley Brown:

> My editing of *Cosmopolitan* is almost completely intuitive. No logic whatever enters into one's decision to like or not like an article. You just have a feeling that it will work or it won't, that it is boring or it isn't, all instinctual. . . .
> I think I'm very good about spotting who is phony or sincere, lying or dissembling, secure or frightened. . . . Whatever

it [intuition] is, it doesn't seem to me that any successful professional person can operate without it.

Among the most enthusiastic proponents of intuition is Ed Asner, for many years the beloved Lou Grant of the "Mary Tyler Moore Show" and now star of his own show, "Lou Grant," on CBS. He told me:

> As an actor, one is always confronted (if one is lucky) with where to make one's choices . . . which one of these roles should I essay? Do I pass up the money here for the quality of the role there? Do I pass up the quality of the role there for the audience numbers that will be reached here? Call it gut feeling, call it intuition, we as actors are always bringing it into play.

And from Dore Schary, the writer and screenwriter, comes this story:

> Many years ago I sat down to write a letter to Mrs. Roosevelt outlining my idea for a play about FDR. I had been referring to it in my mind and in notes as The Roosevelt Story. As I sat down to write, it occurred to me that I needed a title. I spent a few moments thinking about one, couldn't get anything I liked and said, "The hell with it. I'll do it later." I lifted the sheet on which I had been scribbling off the pad and wrote, without any hesitation, the title, "Sunrise at Campobello." It was Thornton Wilder who said that writing simply comes down the arm and into the pen. Maybe in writing that's about all we know — intuition.

And from Rise Stevens, the former mezzo-soprano star of the Metropolitan Opera, comes this poignant note: "Intuition plays an enormous part in one's life and career. Without it as far as I am concerned, one would be a lost soul."

In the field of journalism, intuition is crucial. Journalist Roscoe Drummond told me:

I have always considered intuition the highest and most reliable source of thinking. It has guided me on numerous occasions, once when I abandoned the idea of a law career when I was in high school and chose newspaper work; another time when I decided to try to make my career with the *Christian Science Monitor*, which I served for thirty years.

His intuition still serves him well in his continuing career as a syndicated columnist for the *Los Angeles Times*.

In medicine, teaching, or any of the professions, intuition is a valuable tool. Doctors, who depend on empirical tests, X rays, and observations, lean heavily on logic and reason in their work. But Dr. Leonard Plaine, urologist and professor at New York University Hospital, confided: "A doctor often finds that all the tests are inconclusive and only his intuition can guide him to the answers he needs."

Dr. Warren Cohn, my personal physician, a fine internist from Wilton, Connecticut, heartily agrees and adds, "How do I feel about intuition? We learn a tremendous amount from the books, but what happens in our office is often very different. Medicine is an art rather than a science. Intuition is a vital factor in taking care of our patients."

In law, Justice Oliver Wendell Holmes, one of our most famous judges, wrote as far back as 1905: "General propositions do not decide concrete cases. The decision will depend on a judgment or intuition more subtle than any articulate major premise."

And in teaching, Dr. J. Douglas Brown of Princeton University once wrote:

Excellence in teaching, as well as excellence in scholarship, requires intuition. A liberal university is always seeking men who have this quality, even though the precise term is seldom used. Perhaps it is the pragmatic strain in American culture which reserves "intuition" for poets and women, and assumes that those responsible for the important affairs of the world should be logical at all times. All one can counter is that the discovery of most of the great ideas of the world and the contributions of its most influential leaders involved intuition and not logic alone. A university can disregard this fact only at the risk of losing the excitement and vitality which are its peculiar heritage.

And perhaps the most respected mathematical genius and renowned scientist of our time, Albert Einstein, believed that "an idea is the product of intuition as well as reason."

HOW TO GET LUCKY

After you have been in the business world for a few years, you will find that much of economic success depends on what appears to be luck. Chance-taking is an intrinsic part of the business world. In the garment business, the entrepreneur's ability to anticipate the season's big fashion trend will determine whether he makes a profit or goes bankrupt. Auto dealers have to know whether to stock up on small cars or big ones. Farmers must divine which crop to plant because it will be in short supply. The builder must decide whether it is time to build more expensive houses, if, in fact, the tract bungalow market has been saturated. The aspiring restaurateur has to guess whether what the world needs most is another Mexican food restaurant.

Some business people appear to guess right again and again. They keep taking chances and winning. But it is not dumb luck. *The intuitive factor gives them a powerful edge.* They have the ability to calculate the odds based on information processed at an intuitive level.

As Herman W. Lay, president of Frito-Lay, once said, "When it comes down to the long record and the hard facts, *you* are your own luck. What we ordinarily call luck may really be a bit of chance — something unprepared for and unexpected — but usually there's more to it than that. I think it is partly intuition, which is a kind of thinking that goes on when we aren't aware of it, when we aren't consciously working at our thinking. I believe too that it is a sense of timeliness you develop that tells you *when* to make your move."

Success favors the chance-taker. Too many of us think that chance-taking is foolish and unnecessary. The pervasive philosophy of those who look for security is "Why take chances? Play it safe!" Because *success favors the chance-takers*, that's why! Nothing ventured, nothing gained. Expand that to read, *Life* favors the chance-taker. Timidity does not make for progress or happiness.

Risk is inherent in every aspect of making a living. Here is an example: Barry R. is at the trainee-level in an administrative job. He sees a way in which his work can be done more efficiently. Should he tell his supervisor? The answer is not an automatic yes. If he is unlucky, his supervisor could be an insecure person who might interpret Barry's suggestion as a threat to his own job, and thus Barry would inadvertently acquire an enemy.

When faced with taking a chance in business, I recommend you do everything possible to analyze and weigh all the facts and figures. Gather all the data you can, use all your judgmental faculties, and even if you think the choice is now obvious, *check your intuition* before you take the final step. If your intuitive sense says no when your reason and judgment say *yes*, wait, gather more data, and consider your choices again.

THE VITAL TOOL

Your intuitive system is a "bullshit detector." It bypasses the surface image, the pose, the fabrication, and picks up the *real* message a person is beaming at you. It gets at the truth even when the dissembler himself isn't aware of what he's doing. Intuition enables you to judge what people *really* want, no matter what they say. And when you know what they really want, it is that much easier to respond properly and get results that are satisfactory to both of you.

My father told this story: When he came to the United States from South Africa after a brief sojourn in London, he had no trouble getting a job at Marshall Field, the Chicago department store, because of his British accent and manners. He was placed in the ladies shoe department, but to everyone's surprise, including his own, he did very poorly. He just couldn't seem to make very many sales of the elegant shoes carried by Marshall Field.

One day, while fitting a woman who told him she wore size 7B, he inadvertently brought out 8B. Oblivious of the size, she loved the shoes and bought several pairs. My father got an intuitive flash, and from then on, he always brought out a larger size than the one the woman asked for. He became the number-one salesman in that department because he had broken through a wall of self-delusion: In an age when small feet were a sign of elegance, he allowed the women to have their vanity but still, due to his discretion, wear comfortable shoes. Years later, he referred to that incident as a "lucky idea" — but wasn't it really his intuitive insight into the vanity of that age?

OTHER WAYS INTUITION CAN HELP

Intuition can help you make more money. It provides you with answers to problems at work that reason alone could never solve. For instance:

Is this a potential buyer or just a window-shopper? It is most important for any salesperson to recognize a serious shopper and to differentiate him or her from the one who is "just looking." The one who is "just looking" may be using you to pass the time, asking you to show him item after item, but never intending to buy. It is just wasted effort for you, and you may also be unable to give attention to a buying customer.

But I've also known top salespeople who handle this matter skillfully, firmly believing that *every* customer is really looking to buy even though they may not know it themselves. This kind of salesperson can, if he has the time, change a "just looking" customer into a buying customer by intuiting what unconscious need brought that person into the store in the first place. A supersaleswoman in a top jewelry store told me this story:

"An elderly lady came in one day and asked to see some charms. She said she wanted to buy one for her granddaughter's charm bracelet. She was frail and slow-moving and I think if we had been terribly busy I might have had a tendency to overlook her — a charm isn't a large purchase in a jewelry store. But I had time that day. I said, 'Look around and tell me if there is anything else you would like to see.' On impulse, I took out a large diamond-studded cocktail ring, the size of a golf ball, and put it on my own hand, to show her. 'Pretty, isn't it?' I said. She was fascinated, and I must have spent an hour showing her the other diamond rings. Well, to make a long story short, she ended up buying a five-thousand-dollar diamond ring — plus the five-ninety-eight charm for her granddaughter.

"It turned out she was a wealthy widow and had unconsciously decided to buy herself something that her stingy but well-off husband never did when he was alive. She had never got a diamond engagement ring and the large ones I had shown her looked good against her elderly hands. She left, a happy and delighted lady, and I'll bet she is going to be the envy of her bridge club or church social club.

"How did I intuit what to show her? I haven't a clue. Maybe I had unconsciously seen her glance at the diamond ring display case, but I wouldn't swear to it. I bet a young and inexperienced salesperson would have let her go out with just a charm."

The intuitive salesperson knows when to listen, which item the customer really prefers, what reassurances the customer needs ("A diamond is a good investment these days," the supersaleswoman above had said to her widow, "and you can leave it as an heirloom to your granddaughter."), and when to close the sale. All supersalespeople are intuitive.

Is he kidding or is he serious? Almost all interaction between people can be broken down into action and reaction, thrust and parry, especially in the business world. Sometimes there is no clear way you can tell what the intention of the speaker is except through intuition. There may be no clue in his face or his manner when he says, "Didn't you get enough sleep last night?" Is he intimating you aren't on your toes? Or is he concerned about your being overworked?

Is John really a good friend? Out in the business world, knowing whether a person is a friend or an enemy can be crucial to your career. It may also help you decipher actions that might otherwise be puzzling. Alas, it is often difficult, in a business context, to tell friend from enemy; both may come across the same way. For example, the colleague who helps you with your work so you won't have to stay so late: a friend might do it to make it easier for you, an enemy might do it to make points with the boss.

Start with the premise that you don't trust anyone until he or she has proven himself trustworthy. *"Trustworthy" has to be earned.* Innocent until proved guilty is okay for the criminal courts; in business assume nobody is trustworthy until proven so.

Is my personal style or manner hurting me in my job? How you look or talk is often as important as how well you work. In a large organization, the people at the top may see you every day but never actually observe how efficient you are at your job. They form an impression of you from surface qualities, and often these are the only guidelines they have.

Dressing up can sometimes be as bad as looking sloppy. Early in my career, there was one colleague who always dressed impeccably, yet made no points with the boss by it. If his intuition had been operating in high gear, he might have realized that the boss hated fashion plates: He himself was a shirt-sleeves man who had come up the hard way.

STREET SMARTS

The intelligence quotient (IQ) tests, so widely used in academia, supposedly evaluate your ability to learn and they are sometimes used to determine which schools, jobs, and professions will be open to you.

Unfortunately, the IQ tests only test one half of your brain, the reasoning left brain; they practically ignore the right brain, your nonverbal intelligence. It is as though your vision were tested by examining only one eye and then assuming the other is the same.

Winston Churchill, Albert Einstein, and Thomas Edison all did poorly in school and probably would have performed abysmally on an IQ test had it been used in their day. Yet each proved successful in the world; each of these men contributed enormously to our society. We all know people like them who did not do well academically but thrived when they were catapulted into "real life." They are probably right-brain-oriented rather than left-brain-oriented, and they flourish out of academia where the left brain is king. Once the artificial, rigid environment of classroom instruction is out of the way, intuition becomes a powerful force in coping with the real world.

In our big cities, there is a special kind of awareness that makes for survival on the streets. It is an ability to recognize danger and see things as they really are, not as they appear. This kind of savvy, known as "street smarts," cannot be learned from books. It is generally found in people who have had little formal education and whose livelihoods depend on being able to work the streets: shoeshine boys, taxicab drivers, hucksters, peddlers, truckers, door-to-door salesmen, newsboys. Perhaps their minimal formal education accounts for their strongly developed intuitive sense. They must rely on their own perceptions and evaluations, and so, early on, they discover the value of their intuitive signals. In the streets, there is little time for reflection — instant action and reaction may be necessary — and so the intuitive plays its important role.

People who are successful on Wall Street are said to have "street smarts," with a capital S because a similar instinct is needed on this street too. No amount of book learning will ensure success on Wall Street. You need another kind of savvy — derived from intuition.

CAUTION — PITFALLS AHEAD

In mastering the art of intuition you must be mindful that most people are reason-oriented.

Just as important as tapping your intuition is learning how to present the new insights it provides. Like any powerful tool, intuition must be used with skill and discretion. When dealing with other people, particularly in business, every conclusion you come to ought to have evidence or logic to support it. If you have partners or business associates, prepare logical reasons for your decisions, even though you know that you are being guided by intuition. Saying that you just "had a feeling" you should sell immediately or that your intuition told you not to make the deal will not be sufficient, since most people are primarily rational. You will find it easier, and more palatable to your colleagues, to find a logical reason for the action you want to take. Be as strong in your decisions as you like, but be mindful with whom and when you share your true decision-making process.

RESULTS ARE MORE IMPORTANT THAN SWEAT

Do not barter away your intuitive talent too cheaply. In the marketplace there are two basic guidelines used when computing fair compensation for anything:

1. How much does what you are selling cost you in time, energy, effort?
2. How much does the other party benefit from what you furnish?

Most of us are familiar with the first guideline because we measure how much we have to do on a job to determine how much money we should receive in payment. If you work eight hours at a job you think is worth $4 an hour, you will expect to get $32 for the work. If you get only $25, you doubtless feel exploited; if you get $40, you think you have done well.

But under the second guideline, hours and hard work have nothing to do with the payment you should expect. The yardstick here is "benefit conferred," or what is it worth to the buyer or employer?

You can easily see that the fee for a surgeon cannot be measured by the time he spends at the operation, or the lawyer for the time he spends telling you "If you do that, you'll go to jail," or the professional baseball player for the time and effort he uses to hit a home run, or the concert pianist who fills the hall and plays for fifty minutes, or the broker who sells a house with a few telephone calls. There are many, many jobs where the fee is determined by the benefit to the recipient rather than the "sweat" expended.

In all these occupations, the person performing the work

is paid for a special skill, knowledge, or experience. Whenever you use your intuitive sense, you are using a very special talent. It is the product of your unconscious knowledge, experience, and skills garnered over a lifetime. Sometimes quite priceless when you consider the benefit it creates!

Intuitive insight often hits you like a flashbulb going off. In an instant, an idea that is invaluable for your employer or associates lights up in your mind. When this happens, you should, of course, be suitably rewarded. You must, therefore, carefully time and present your ideas to ensure appropriate compensation. Remember: *Results* and *solutions* are more important than time and effort.

NO BONUS FOR THE INTUITIVE ANSWER

Some years ago I was elected director of a small public company. Soon after, there were months when the monthly board meetings were canceled without explanation. When the board finally met, the president, who looked worried, passed out financial reports and explained that the company would show a very large loss in its annual statement. That was particularly unfortunate as it was the company's first annual report after going public. The repercussions could cause a spate of lawsuits.

I looked around the boardroom and realized that all the other officer-directors had known about the problem and that the company attorney and auditors knew it too. The gloom was thick as the attorney described the exposure of the company and the liabilities of the individual directors.

Still listening with one ear, I began to check the balance sheet, the profit and loss statements, and the accountant's suggested financial notes. Suddenly, the proverbial light went on in my head and I saw a way to solve the whole problem. It was an intuitive flash. Quickly I checked mentally to see whether certain steps could be taken so that a different, approved, accounting treatment could be used for recasting the figures so that the loss would not appear in this first annual report. It would give the business an opportunity to straighten itself out.

I interrupted the meeting and said, "Just a minute — I've got an idea; it may be the answer to the problem."

I went on to explain in detail what I had in mind. It took a little while to sink in, but soon they were all nodding in agreement. When the meeting broke up, several of the men congratulated me: "How the hell did you come up with that answer?" they wanted to know. I felt good, but I really should have been kicking myself.

About a year later the company began to reap the results of its earlier efforts and made tremendous profits. I was not surprised, I was even a little pleased, when the president announced that bonuses would be given. The president and all the officers were taken care of. However, I was disappointed, to say the least, to find that my name was not included among those to get bonuses. I restrained myself until the meeting was over and then I cornered the president alone.

"Why didn't I get a bonus like the others?"

"Why, Fisher," he said, "we're all hardworking employees working for the success of the company. You're just a director, and of course, you get your director's fee."

"Don't you think I made a very important contribution during this past year?"

"What do you mean?"

"I mean coming up with the idea of how to handle the financials so there wouldn't be a rash of lawsuits from our banks and stockholders."

"Aw, come on, you came up with that idea in two minutes. It was a perfectly obvious answer to the problem. Anyone could have seen it."

It may have been obvious, but none of the officers, other directors, accountants, or lawyers had found the answer during all the months the meetings had been postponed. By coming up with the answer too quickly, I cheapened it. In the president's eyes it didn't involve very much work or effort and so it couldn't be worth much.

I learned my lesson, and I've set it down in some detail for you to learn from my experience. Your intuition, which is the result of millions of bits of information absorbed over a lifetime, enables you to find solutions to complicated problems. When these intuitive skills are used for someone else's profit, be sure that you are paid for "benefit conferred."

THE INTUITIVE REVIEW

You have learned to prepare yourself for invoking the intuitive message. However, you do not have to reserve this decoupling of conscious drive for the twilight zones in your day. Do it any time you need intuitive input. Find a quiet spot and "turn down" your left brain activity. Then review any problem or experience you want to understand more deeply, by running the points or scenes over again in your mind.

When I have a business problem that calls for a quick response, I often tell my associates that I need a few minutes to think before I make my decision — *but I don't "think," I intuit.* I go off by myself even if it is only to another room, close my eyes, go through the relaxation exercise briefly, blot out all other thoughts, and gently review all aspects of the deal. Though it sounds simplistic, it works; it is astonishing how many times the answer comes through clear as a bell.

11

You Can
Stay Healthy

It has been estimated that sixty to seventy-five percent of all medical problems are caused or aggravated by anxiety, fear, pain, and depression. That many physical diseases are induced by the patient's psyche is no secret to doctors. In fact, the term *psychosomatic* describes real diseases whose genesis is in the mind. This does not include those diseases that are imaginary, "all in the mind." An arm that is paralyzed because of a mental problem is just as incapacitating as an arm that is immobile because the nerves have been severed.

Norman Cousins's best-selling book, *Anatomy of an Illness,* tells of his decision to take his very real illness into his own hands after doctors had given up on him. Having read that unhappiness exacerbates illness, he theorized that joy would then, presumably, make one well. He took a room in a hotel (convinced that hospitals today are no place for a sick person) and, prescribing massive doses of good humor for himself, spent his days watching comedy on television and reading humorous books. After much rest and lots of Vitamin C,

Cousins is alive today and lecturing at a medical school on the use of happiness in the healing process.

SPONTANEOUS REMISSION

"Spontaneous remission" means that the patient got well for no reason known to medical science. But your intuition may know all about spontaneous remission. If you are ill, your intuitive system may very well be working right this moment on a "remission" that may, in the end, appear to be "spontaneous" to your doctor.

Intuition can help you anticipate an illness, diagnose the problem, and get you well. It is invaluable in helping you pick the right doctor, recognize illness in a person close to you, or even, as some assert, produce a cure for cancer.

Haven't you at one time or another figured out why you were sick? I can still hear my dad saying, "I'll have to stop going to those pep-talk meetings at the office. They give me a headache every time." One young friend gets stomach cramps about an hour before the high school swimming meets — he hates competing. Another girl gets a skin rash every time she has a personal crisis. There are countless examples of people who have not only diagnosed themselves but also succeeded in curing themselves.

When illness is diagnosed, the doctor and the patient must work hand in hand in the healing process. The physician should be a *guide* rather than a final authority, and a guide who takes into account the intuitive feelings of the patient about the course of treatment.

All of us have intuitively diagnosed and prescribed for ourselves: "I should get more exercise," "I should lose some weight," "I need more sleep," "I should take a vacation," "I don't eat right," "I am too nervous, probably too much coffee,"

"Smoking is going to kill me," "She's no good for me, I should break away."

All of these common statements are actually (1) observations of a present state that interferes with health, and (2) indicators of a method for correction. And each of these diagnoses and prescriptions for cure displays the fine hand of intuition, which brings the condition into your conscious mind, tugging at your mental sleeve.

PICA

A powerful example of how intuition operates to keep the body on an even keel is the phenomenon known as Pica. Dr. Allan Cott tells about a distraught mother who brought her daughter to him with a severe and seemingly insolvable problem. It had developed as soon as the child, Carol, was able to crawl: She ate nonedibles. A pediatrician had told the mother that she would outgrow it. But one day, when Carol was at the creeping stage, she started to lick the top of a can of Comet cleanser. As she grew, her appetite also grew, and came to include candles, crayons, chalk, and graphite. She loved all cosmetics, especially lipstick. When she played out of doors, her appetite ran to spoonfuls of dirt and sand, cigarettes, matches, and paper, all of which she chewed and swallowed with the relish of a hungry child.

Carol was demonstrating a condition known as Pica, a craving for nonedible, unnatural food. Cases of Pica have been reported throughout man's history, and doctors have speculated that it is the individual's way of coping with a critical mineral deficiency. After appropriate tests, Dr. Cott treated Carol with vitamins and micronutrients, and within a few months the child had lost her strange eating compulsion.

Pica is a dramatic example of how the intuitive system works to keep us healthy and alive. Surely, the patient does not consciously know that the body requires certain minerals, but the intuitive system does and tries to solve the problem.

THE INTUITIVE PATIENT

The patient himself can be a most important factor in diagnosing and healing. Use your intuition to pick up clues that may lead to a sharper diagnosis or indicate which course to take in treatment. Report your observations to your doctor for verification. If your doctor ignores or sloughs off your observations and comments, get another doctor.

T.V.H., though now remarkably healthy, has had some ten successful surgical operations during the twenty-five years we've known each other. Recently I had lunch with him and we discussed illnesses and doctors. He told me, "I never submit to a doctor's examination until I've told him in the most minute detail everything I can about what *I* think is wrong. Believe it or not, many of them told me that I gave them important clues to the diagnosis — and a course of treatment as well."

Then he continued: "I've just come from the dentist who was supposed to operate on me for an abscessed tooth. I said, 'Doc, I think the abscess is starting to subside,' He laughed and said, 'Everyone gets better when they are in the dentist's chair.' But he decided to take a closer look before proceeding, and said, 'It does look a little better. Let's hold off until tomorrow, and we'll see.' 'I bet you lunch,' my friend said, 'that he doesn't have to operate. But if I hadn't spoken up, I'd be home in bed right now with cut and stitched gums — or worse, one tooth less.'"

As it turned out, T.V.H. was right. The dentist didn't have to operate. And I had to buy him lunch!

Even more dramtic was the experience of Anne Ziff, an editor and author of children's books, who told me this story:

"My intuition saved my daughter Amy's life. I suppose you didn't know, but my first child was stillborn. I had carried beyond full term and the doctors had to induce birth. When the baby was delivered, the placenta was flat; there had not been enough oxygen and food to sustain life. It was very traumatic. Fortunately I conceived again, and Debbie was born a normal, healthy baby. Two years later I became pregnant again, but had a sense of 'something' being wrong throughout the pregnancy. I became more and more apprehensive as the pregnancy advanced, and insisted that my obstetrician run certain nonroutine tests. He assured me that the baby was quite alive but very small. I intuitively felt that he was wrong and that the baby was a proper size and due. Finally, thirteen days before my due date, the tests showed there was trouble. I was told to go into the hospital for a more thorough checkup plus constant bed rest.

"They gave me all kinds of tests, and after another examination by a specialist I was told that the baby was tiny and still had a considerable time to go, that to induce labor would be a mistake, and that the test results would be read in six days. I was to have complete bed rest in the interim.

"I went berserk — I started to throw things — screamed, et cetera. The nurses were frightened and tried to calm me down, but my fears and anger were not, seemingly, rational. Ultimately (nearly two days later) my doctor said that if my husband and I would sign waivers he would do a Caesarean delivery the next day. I immediately calmed down. We signed the papers and a wonderful, healthy daughter, Amy, was born.

"When I woke, I found my doctor hovering over my bed. There were tears in his eyes and he said, 'Anne, you were not crazy! If we had let it go another three days she would have been dead. The placenta could not have sustained her life another forty-eight hours.'

"Taking the chance of *acting* on this intuitive conviction saved her life!"

SELECTING A DOCTOR

Never pick a doctor or any professional person unless you get an intuitive okay: Your right brain awareness may be saving your life. The empathetic doctor is more likely not only to make a correct diagnosis but also to carefully follow the course of your treatment and to react to your changing condition. He will be more sensitive to your needs and your progress; he will have an awareness of the total you, not just the clinical condition written down on your bed chart.

THERAPIES THAT MAKE USE OF INTUITION

There are many little-known healing methods that use the intuitive part of the brain. Although some of these go back to antiquity, they do not all have the unqualified acceptance of the medical profession. A short survey is included here because, unlike some of the dangerous medications and treatments that *are* approved by doctors, these healing methods are relatively harmless. Most can be followed at home, alone, and cost nothing. In most cases the only side effect is disappointment if they do not work for you. You may wish to investigate them further.

THE USE OF HYPNOSIS AND SELF-HYPNOSIS IN HEALING

Hypnosis is the only one of the therapies considered here that has been officially accepted by the medical and psychiatric establishment as a method of treatment. In 1969, both the American Medical Association and the American Psychiatric Association issued policy statements to this effect.

Nevertheless, because of its early connection with stage tricks, many people still think of hypnosis as questionable and discount its effectiveness. Not only is hypnosis effective, but it is also safe and has helped many people overcome their need for drug treatment for pain and anxiety.

J. E. was troubled by insomnia and consulted Dr. Herbert Spiegel, a respected staff physician at Columbia Presbyterian Hospital in New York. She tells this story:

"I was convinced that I was not going to be a good subject for hypnosis. But I knew that insomnia is usually psychogenic — that is, produced by the mind — and not physical, and I also knew that I didn't want to spend five years and thousands of dollars in psychoanalysis to find out why. I needed to sleep well *tonight*.

"Dr. Spiegel first questioned me closely about my insomnia and why I wanted to rid myself of the condition. (Later on, I found out he was establishing how motivated I was.) Then he gave me a little lecture on how normal sleep is, how the body knows to take rest when it needs to, how a regular sleep time is important, and so on. Then he taught me how to enter a trance state and said, 'When I count to ten, your left arm will rise.'

"I thought, 'Well, he's such a nice guy I hate to disappoint him, but no way is my arm going to go up on anybody's command.' 'Ten!' he said, and to my astonishment, *my left arm went up in the air!* To this day, I don't understand how it happened. I know I didn't consciously will it to. My instant reaction, observing my arm, was 'Oh my, look what's happening!'

"Dr. Spiegel fed into my now highly receptive mind all of the things he had said when I was not under hypnosis. Then he instructed me to come out of the trance. Later he taught me how to hypnotize myself anywhere at any time. The punch line of this story is that I now have 'thirty-second insomnia' — I hit the pillow and am asleep in thirty seconds."

In the process of researching this book, I talked to Dr. Spiegel and he told me, "The highly hypnotizable person tends to be intuitive. By the same token, the very intuitive person is highly hypnotizable. But though intuition is important, it is only one factor in determining whether a person will be a good subject for hypnosis. Motivation is important. Many people intuitively shift into their hypnotic capacity from time to time and don't even realize it."

The psychodynamics involved in hypnosis relax the subject so deeply that his conscious is placed in a recessive role and the intuitive becomes dominant. It is later able to implement the instructions fed during hypnosis without interference from conscious fears or resistance. Many hospitals today will recommend a physician, psychiatrist, or psychologist on their staff who uses hypnosis.

THE PHENOMENON OF VISUALIZATION

Paracelsus, a Renaissance physician, considered the father of modern medicine, believed that people could be healed by their own thoughts. A remnant of this belief has persisted within the medical profession. We've all heard the melodramatic final statement of the attending physician on television: "It's all up to the patient now."

In their book *Seeing with the Mind's Eye*, Mary Samuels and Dr. Mike Samuels discuss self-healing by visualization, whereby the patient creates a mental picture of the afflicted part of his body and scans his mind to discover what is causing the ailment. The authors point out that man has used visualization from the earliest time to help in diagnosis and treatment. The Babylonian, Egyptian, Greek, East Indian, and ancient Oriental civilizations all used visualization techniques for healing.

Here's how it works: Visualize in your mind's eye the part of your body that troubles you. In a relaxed way, focus all your attention on this mind-picture. Be ready for and receptive to any intuitive message you may get. As you scan one part of your body with the intuitive camera of your mind, you will get, on your picture screen, clues that may aid in diagnosis. Be receptive to whatever pops into your head seemingly out of nowhere. No matter how superficially irrelevant, it may contain your answer. Here are a few examples of patient problems that were successfully dealt with by this technique.

Spitting blood. A middle-aged man was very upset to find blood in his mouth for several days on arising. He visualized a wine press with grape juice oozing from its sides, and realized the blood came from his gums as he ground his teeth in his sleep. This was confirmed by his dentist who treated his gums.

Pain in foot. An elderly executive with a cramped arch in his foot visualized a scene of someone being hanged. Upon inspection, he found the elastic on the top of his high-rise stockings was too tight and had cut his circulation.

Nausea. A young woman closed her eyes and tried to visualize why her stomach was in turmoil. A quaint fishing village came into her mind. She remembered then that she had had dubious salmon for lunch.

For further information on this technique, the Samuelses' book, *Seeing with the Mind's Eye,* is recommended.

AUTOGENIC THERAPY

The proponents of Autogenic Therapy believe that you can learn to control and use your body's built-in mechanisms for self-healing through visualization and its logical follow-through — the setting in motion of the body's own self-regenerating, self-regulating capability. In Autogenic Therapy the patient is programmed, or programs himself, to cope with his specific illness.

For example, if you suffer from cold hands, you will try to imagine you are in contact with your hands. You concentrate and repeat a given formula phrase: "My hands are getting warmer." You may be quite pleased to find that your hands are indeed getting warmer.

For a stomach ailment, you may repeat, "I am at peace," or "My stomach is calm," or whatever is appropriate to your specific problem. Particular exercises designed to induce relaxation and bring about psychological changes that will promote self-healing are also prescribed for the individual.

Does it work? Autogenic Therapy has been widely used in Europe for years. It has been found to produce good results in a number of ailments, including ulcers, gastritis, gall bladder attacks, irritated colon, hemorrhoids, constipation, obesity, heart attacks, angina, high blood pressure, headaches, asthma, diabetes, thyroid disease, arthritis, and low back pain. It is also used as an adjunct in chemotherapy, surgery, psychology, and dentistry.

All of the therapies mentioned work to some degree, depending on the nature of your illness and the limitations imposed by the physical world — you cannot, for instance, will yourself to fly — but you can will yourself to be calm. Even doctors will admit, within what is physically possible, the body is its own best healer.

12

Using
Intuition in Sex

In all their research on the orgasm, famed sex researchers Masters and Johnson have never been able to pin down why an individual is attracted to one person and not to another. Sexual attraction remains a mysterious phenomenon, unlikely to be explained anytime soon by science and technology. The choice of a sex partner appears to be an intuitive function.

Is it safe to rely on your intuition in choosing a sexual or marriage partner? From all we know at this time, it seems the *only* way. One woman who worked in the office of a computer dating service told me: "No matter how perfectly we paired off a couple in relation to height, religion, race, likes and dislikes, the actual physical meeting was the decisive factor. And no matter how much they *should* have liked each other, we could never predict whether they would or wouldn't. Nine times out of ten, when the couple should have been drawn to each other because they had so much in common, they took an instant dislike to each other. We just couldn't predict how they would react."

A sexual "turn-on" is not a rational decision. It is created initially by your intuitive system, which picks up and processes sexual stimuli as well as your own outgoing sexual messages. The intuitive first triggers the sexual response of your body and then sends messages of arousal to your conscious.

Have you, for instance, ever been surprised at the engorgement and excitement of your sexual organs before you had a sexual thought? Sexual arousal starts before you are consciously aware that something is "turning you on."

FINDING THAT SPECIAL STRANGER

Julius Fast, author of *Body Language*, tells about a young man named Mike who had the inexplicable talent of arriving at a party and within half an hour pinpointing the girl he would end up taking home that evening. Mike was not especially good-looking or above average in intelligence, or a smooth talker. But, Fast points out, he had a "sixth sense when it came to women. If a girl was available that evening, Mike would find her. Mike sent out sexual messages by the way he stood, walked, moved, and made gestures.

Body language is certainly an important communication subsystem that is used intuitively; you cannot really control it no matter how much you try. Compared with the intuitive system as a whole, however, body language is like a tom-tom drum competing with a satellite communications network. The explanation for Mike's success, I believe, is not simply his body language, but probably a complex array of intuitive signals. Mike seems to be an intuitive person who has sharpened his intuitive awareness in the sexual sphere.

Of course, women have identical intuitive sexual senses when it comes to finding an attractive man. Although the example below is of a man, it also applies to women — when the roles are reversed.

You are at a party, the lights are low, the room is humming with conversation, you look around to find someone who might interest you. A woman chatting with someone else in a corner looks interesting. The more you observe her, the more interested you are. Your attraction to her might be based on the following:

1. *Past good experience.* If your best sexual experiences have been with buxom brunettes, you may find yourself being intuitively drawn to such women without consciously seeking them out.

2. *Familiarity.* Your attraction to tall thin blondes is not a mystery if your mother and sisters are tall thin blondes. Your sense of the beauty of the opposite sex is usually established in childhood and any conscious decision you may make to "come on" to a charming redhead are to no avail. You can't "reason" with intuition.

3. *Availability.* The woman chatting with someone else has sent out signals of availability that have been received by your intuitive. It can be the way she has looked at you or the desultory way she is paying attention to her companion. Your intuition has picked these up.

4. *Detecting Interest on the part of the other person.* She has also radiated a message of interest to you. Is it the way she has looked you up and down? Have her eyes returned to you again and again? Has she turned her body toward you? Your intuition has noted her interest in you, and like most people, you respond to people who are interested in you.

5. *Answering an unconscious need.* You have always had a need to be seen with an attractive woman, it seems to counteract your feelings of low self-esteem, though logically you know you ought to be just as interested in an intelligent plain woman. Your intuition knows your priorities. This woman's physical attractiveness draws you to her.

Ought you then try to meet the woman? Since the whole scenario so far has been wholly intuitive, you will probably make a move toward her at the first opportunity. To go against your intuition at this point would certainly be folly. If you learn from Mike, you will not hesitate for a moment.

For a woman, the final stage in this game plan may be slightly more subtle. Despite women's liberation, our social attitudes often inhibit your making the decisive move. But if your intuition is working, you will know after a few minutes whether the man is interested or just being polite, and you will know — intuitively — how to encourage him or gracefully move on.

These intuitive principles apply not only in group situations but in one-to-one encounters as well. A bachelor I know related this experience:

"One Sunday I went with a blind date to an art museum. She turned out to be OK, but she really didn't turn me on. As we were going from room to room, looking at paintings, I accidentally bumped into a woman in charge of one wing — no stunning beauty, but attractive. I chatted with her for a while until she said, 'I think your wife is calling you.' 'She's not my wife, but thank you,' I said.

"I took my date home and forgot about the whole thing. Then, on Thursday afternoon, I suddenly remembered the woman. I called the museum, described the floor and section I wanted, and finally got her. I said, 'You probably don't remember me. I was in your section last Sunday ——'

"She interrupted with, 'Of course I do. What took you so long? I've been waiting to hear from you.' That was the beginning of one of the most torrid affairs of my life and I can't account for how it happened."

FINDING A PARTNER IS ONLY THE BEGINNING

You've found her, or him. The brunette in the corner has turned out to be, as your intuition so rightly alerted you, interested and available. Don't abandon you intuitive messages at this point.

Shere Hite, in *The Hite Report*, quotes dozens of bitter complaints by women about the insensitivity, egocentricity, and lack of concern of their male lovers. The women were really talking about the lack of intuitive sexual sensitivity of their partners.

Dr. Mildred Hope Witkin, sex therapist with the Payne-Whitney Institute in New York, said at a recent forum: "Trying to solve sexual problems by logic is sheer folly. The sex gestalt of each human is unique and complex. When a lover is added to the equation, the possibilities for problems are compounded. *Fortunately we each have an innate sensitivity which helps us find the right answers.* The therapist's job is to help remove blocks and inhibitors of that intuitive awareness" (emphasis mine).

We cannot dismiss the influence of the five conscious senses in the act of lovemaking: The sight of your sex partner, the touch, the fragrance of his or her skin, the sounds of his or her pleasure, yes, even the taste of your partner are aspects of lovemaking that you can maximize with the help of your intuition.

Intuition tunes you in to the *unspoken* needs of your partner. The highly intuitive person is sexually sensitive as well. The act of lovemaking is, for all intents and purposes, nonverbal, and communication during each phase must therefore be intuitive. Although it is not within the scope of this book to give you explicit sexual instructions, consider one phase of lovemaking in which the partners often fail to achieve communication. A student once asked, "Why is it that most men cannot tell when a woman is nearing orgasm?"

Why indeed? Although women ordinarily do not announce when they are approaching orgasm, there are nonverbal indications that are sometimes so strong that only a dead man would miss them. In other women, the indications are so subtle they might easily be overlooked. Nevertheless, a man who is attuned to the needs of his partner, who is savoring each step of the lovemaking, will be responsive to each movement, to each accelerated rhythm of his partner and will not be rushed by his own needs. (This also applies equally to a woman's intuitive responsiveness to her male partner.) I recommend The Total Orange exercise at the end of this chapter to help you develop tactile sensitivity and the skill of observation, both of which may be adapted to enhance the sex experience.

Intuition may also alert you to negative factors in a relationship. For example, Doris B. tells a story that demonstrates how infinitely observant and dependable intuition is:

"I have been having a friendly sexual relationship with a man, whom I'll call Louis, for about five years. By 'friendly,' I mean that there were no declarations of love or exclusivity on either side. Lou and I got together once a week, or every two weeks, had dinner, talked, and then had sex. We sometimes talked about the other men or women in our lives, but in all those years, neither of us had had luck meeting anyone else. It was understood that our sexual relationship answered a mutual need: It was a safety valve that prevented us from having to have one-night stands; it was convenient.

"Then one day I met someone with whom I felt I could fall in love. I didn't tell Lou about it, but I turned down several of our Friday nights and made one last-minute cancellation.

"One Friday Lou and I had our usual dinner together and then got into bed. But for once, Lou had a difficult time achieving an erection, and when he finally did he was not able to have an orgasm. We had a cigarette in bed and tried to discuss it, but communication on such a matter is difficult. Lou felt ashamed and insecure. I sensed he was feeling his age that night — he is forty-eight. I tried to pretend it hadn't happened, and if it had, it wasn't important. But of course it was upsetting.

"A few days later I had an intuitive flash and decided to call Lou. Oddly enough, he said he had been wanting to talk to me too. We met for a drink after work and Lou said to me, 'I wasn't my usual self in bed last Friday.' 'Yes, that's true,' I said, wanting to level with him now. 'But it isn't my age,' Lou said, 'It's that I sensed that your interest lay elsewhere.'

" 'I was going to tell you that myself,' I said, incredulous. 'You picked up vibes from me, I'm sure. You see, I haven't had the courage to tell you I've met someone I think I'm falling in love with. I didn't know how to tell you after all these years and all your kindness.' "

Doris had intuitively communicated what she could not communicate verbally, and Lou had reacted to the signals he was getting. Each sensed what was happening to the relationship, but neither had verbalized it. The intuitive, however, is unabashedly honest.

One doesn't hear of sexual problems in the animal world, with the exception of captive animals who, after a long period in captivity, often are unable to reproduce; there are no veterinarians specializing in sex therapy for cattle. Moreover, anthropologists note that there is virtually no sexual dysfunction among primitive peoples except for that imposed physically by accident or illness. It seems to be the civilizing process, with its emphasis on left brain consciousness, that creates sexual failure.

It would be a mistake, however, to think of sex as purely "instinctive" merely because animals do not need Masters and Johnson. Instinct has been defined as unlearned behavior or activity that is adaptive. I believe that what seems to be unlearned consciously is actually learned intuitively. That is, instinct is behavior that is intuitively learned rather than consciously learned, resulting in behavior that *seems* automatic because it's not dictated by the left brain.

If sex were instinctive in humans, we would all have great sex lives — and we know this isn't true for all of us.

If not *instinct* in the classic sense of the word, then what is it? It can only be intuitive. Man was sexual long before he developed language. Ergo, sex was aroused, guided, directed, and controlled by the nonverbal part of the brain long before consciousness, verbalization, and thought. It probably still is to a great extent. It is when the left brain imposes judgment on an intuitive act that sex problems arise.

GUIDED SEX FANTASY

Is he or she the one for you? Your intuition can help you find out before you invest time and psychic energy in trying to develop a relationship. You can do this by means of the Guided Sex Fantasy. It is not a magic formula, but you can obtain some powerful clues from it about whether X is a potential lover for you.

1. Select a quiet spot away from all distraction of sounds, smells, and other sensory stimuli.
2. Lie down in a comfortable position. Wear loose clothing such as pajamas.
3. Do the Basic Warm-up and clear your mind of all thought.
4. Now embark on a dream fantasy: You are in a room that assures you absolute privacy, furnished in the most sensual decor. There is an erotic and subtly stimulating fragrance in the air, and mood music purrs in the background. Alongside of you lies your potential lover. You proceed, in your imagination, to caress and undress him or her.
5. Allow the scenario to unfold on its own now. Give it no direction. What happens? Does your lover respond? Does he or she come alive, caress you in turn? Are you becoming more aroused? Do you experience pleasure and excitement? Are you cooperating and helping him or her? Is the experience pleasurable?
6. When the fantasy has run its course, mentally review

what happened. How do you feel about it? Do you feel that it was wholesome and good? Or are there some reservations, a twinge of anxiety?

The answers to these questions will give you a better understanding about the desirability for you of X as a potential lover. Fantasy factors into your awareness the perceptions that your intuitive has picked up and gives you more details to help with your decision.

This exercise can also be used to help conceptualize how you feel about a potential lover who you know is available. In this case there is little question that X is interested in you; you know that all you have to do is make a move and there would be an inevitable sexual experience. But you are not sure it will be one that you really want. One woman told me that she had followed all the steps in the Guided Sex Fantasy, visualizing a man she had just met, but when it came to visualizing the actual sex act with her potential partner, she drew a blank. She simply could not visualize them making love. A few weeks later she reported that the affair had indeed ended — before it began.

The Guided Sex Fantasy is not an absolute decision maker. It is, rather, a method to assess all the evidence you have, conscious and intuitive, to help you determine whether X is indeed a positive sex choice for you. Be mindful that in the realm of sex, intuition is king (or queen), and when there is indecision, intuition may be the one voice that will tell it to you "like it is."

THE TOTAL ORANGE EXERCISE

Sensuality is to the intuitive what evidence is to the conscious. This requires a little explanation: The uninhibited input from the five senses provides deeper intuitive meaning in the same way that more facts allow you to better reason toward a judgment.

We find many ways to demonstrate how the input from

our five senses is translated into intuitive awareness. Haven't you ever said, or heard someone say, "I feel it in my bones," "I smell something rotten about this deal," "I could taste victory," or "I see a happy ending"? "The bells started to ring when she said, 'Yes.' "

The Total Orange Exercise is designed to introduce you to the possibilities of total sensory immersion into one isolated object, and to demonstrate how a slow, sensual exploration of even the most mundane thing can provide a sensory learning experience when it is done with the uninhibited involvement of each of the senses.

The exercise should take at least ten minutes and you should experience the orange with each of your senses as thoroughly as you can. Many who have completed this exercise have no difficulty transferring it to their next sexual experience.

1. Start with a whole orange. Sit at a table in a quiet, well-lit room. Place the orange on the table in front of you. Look at it, concentrate on its color and shape, allow the color and all its gradations to sink into your consciousness. Note the hills and valleys that make up the skin. Roll the orange on its side. Observe how the colors vary: green, orange, yellow, white, the specks of brown.

2. Pick up the orange and place it against your ear. Listen intently. Tap the orange gently. What do you hear? Allow your finger to rub against the skin. What sound does it produce? Scratch lightly. How does this sound?

3. Take the orange in your hands. Feel the smooth yet dimpled skin. Allow your fingers to explore the navel and stem. Rub the orange gently along your cheek. Roll it over your chin and around your neck. Gently brush it with your lips and feel the texture of its skin with your tongue.

4. Place it back on the table. Close your eyes and cut the skin with your fingernail. Breathe in the fragrance of the

orange. Taste the fragrance. Experience the fragrance as deeply as you can with both your nose and your mouth.

5. Now peel the orange. Feel the oil and sticky moisture on your fingers. Feel the fine spray as the skin breaks. Look at the orange without its skin, notice its color, texture, and shape. Dig the soft center pulp out, examine it. How does it feel, smell, taste? What does it look like? Open up the orange, separate the sections, and observe them. Examine the new color variations, new textures, smells, and taste. Note the pits and everything about them.

6. Pick up one of the sections, feel its size and shape and sponginess. Bite into it. Note the feeling on your tongue and mouth as you press down and squeeze the juice out, the change in the fragrance as you chew, and the sensation of swallowing the juice and pulp.

After you have completed the above very slowly, proceed with the second part of the exercise.

7. Close your eyes and start the Basic Warm-up. When fully relaxed, visualize a giant orange large enough to stand on. You reach down and turn the stem like the hatch on a submarine. It opens up, you look inside, see a ladder and descend into the opening in the orange.

8. Now explore: What do you see? As you climbed down the ladder, did you note that an orange light permeates everything? Did you suddenly become aware that each section of the orange contains its own world? Are the pits perhaps computers or energy sources? Is this a spaceship, a submarine, a fortress? Develop your own sci-fi fantasy that may even involve an adventure. When you are finished, climb out and say farewell to your orange odyssey.

Your understanding of the orange will have expanded to a new plateau. You may find that you and the orange have developed a relationship you've never had before. This technique can be transferred, with very little difficulty for most people, to every aspect of their life.

13

Friends
and
Enemies

A friend enhances the life experience. He shares your successes and failures; he is happy with your triumphs and saddened at
your reverses. A friend is sensitive to your needs and finds in
you a reciprocal sympathetic awareness, understanding, and
openness that create the particular bonding we call friendship.

Although friendship is one of the most intimate and pre-
cious experiences you can enjoy, it also poses some dangers. A
false friend, or a friendship that has gone sour, puts you in a
position of vulnerability: The confidences, hopes, and aspirations you may entrust to a friend can be deadly in the hands of
an enemy.

In this aspect of your life the intuitive is priceless because
it is able to see behind the insincere smile, the surface charm,
the superficial attractiveness. It sloughs aside the outside trappings and deals with the essence of the person. Guile, cunning,
and duplicity are all functions of the reasoning mind, the left
brain. Intuition can no more initiate guile or cunning than can
your eyesight or hearing.

It is irrelevant how many *reasons* there are why someone should be your intimate friend; if your intuition flashes a warning — forget it! You can consider a lesser relationship with that someone — as an acquaintance, or perhaps a business or casual companion. You can do things together for mutual enjoyment or profit. But, you should be on your guard. In time, your intuition may reverse its findings and flash a new message to you, but until then, have more faith in your intuition than in your new acquaintance.

HOW TO TELL A FRIEND FROM AN ENEMY

Put simply, your friends wish you well, your enemies, for whatever reason, consciously or otherwise, wish you ill. Most people in your life are neither friends nor enemies, but have aspects of one or the other or, in some cases, a combination of both. At the same time, love-hate dualism is a feature of most of our relationships — we love a particular friend for his loyalty, but detest his habitual tardiness, love another friend for his humor, but dislike his egocentricity. Alas, our friends are human, as full of strengths and shortcomings as we are.

You can undoubtedly recall at least one twinge of envy at some piece of good luck that befell your friend, or a spasm of jealousy when he found some happiness that left you out. Almost surely that friend will have had similar feelings toward you.

This, however, is very different from the malevolence of an enemy, someone who really wishes you ill. Though an enemy may be dangerous to a greater or lesser extent, most people can cope when the hostility is open and there is no question that he is an enemy.

The really dangerous enemies are those who *seem* to be friends — or are close because they are relatives. You share confidences with them and thereby increase your vulnerability. Sometimes they themselves are unaware of their hidden hostility; this does not make them less dangerous. They think of themselves as "friends" who are acting "for your own good," yet all their actions and advice do you harm.

Tap your intuitive for guidance. Whenever you have a relationship about which you are unsure, go through the relaxation exercises you have learned and when you are fully relaxed, go over the incidents in your life that involve the person in question. Listen for dissonance, pick up trace feelings until you get a clear message. If you come out of this exercise with a feeling that the person is not a friend — is, indeed, an enemy — you should take action to neutralize any harm he could do to you.

Ed. W., a teacher, tells how he learned to deal with the friend-cum-enemy:

"As a young man I was very anxious to be popular and accepted. I was not very discriminating. I leaned over backward to accept everyone as a friend. As a result, many of my friends were not friends at all.

"This was a source of anguish to me. Even when they acted badly I kept trying to convert them into friends, a terrible mistake, but I didn't know this then.

"One day, early in my sophomore year, I was standing around with a group of new classmates. We were finding out about one another between classes. There were several attractive girls in the group and we were talking, kidding around, when one of my so-called friends spotted me and joined the group. I introduced him around as my friend and his first words were, 'What's Ed, the old con man, trying to sell you?'

"I could feel the change in atmosphere. They were embarrassed for me, and the group soon broke up. I was left alone with my 'friend.' I finally got the insight and courage to deal with my phony friend. I said, 'You're no friend of mine, you're a jerk who thinks you can build yourself up by tearing others down. Get lost! Stay away from me.'

"I never spoke to him again. I didn't need an enemy posing as a friend.

"Now, twenty years later, when I get a feeling that someone is my 'enemy,' I think of him as an enemy at once, without any questions. I don't care who he is, relative, business associate, or crony; I guard myself and try to reduce my contact with him. If it is business, I try to bring our affairs to a close and I don't start any new ones. If it is a relative, I taper off contact as much as family obligations allow. If it is a social friend, I try to arrange that we don't mix in the same circles. Sometimes the most effective, though drastic, method is to stop talking to that person altogether. I don't act with hostility or anger, but I do move decisively. In every case where I have stopped talking to a so-called friend, I have never been sorry. In fact, as I review the few total cutoffs I've had to make, I know intuitively that in each case I did the right thing."

THE FRIEND WHO USES YOU

Friendship is a two-way street, but the traffic does not necessarily go in both directions at the same time. There are periods when the flow seems to go only one way, then it reverses and goes the other way.

Very often one friend seems to constantly use the other — for contacts, money, or a shoulder to cry on. The test of a true friendship is whether it is reciprocal. Is the taker also available as a giver? The balance may shift over the years; indeed, it's a rare friendship where this does not happen. The heartbreak comes when after years of giving you find it's a one-way street.

It is wise to intuitively review a friendship from time to time. Your intuitive system with its holistic overview is better able than rationality to assess a friendship.

THE MALE-FEMALE FRIENDSHIP

A new phenomenon is evolving: male-female friendship that is not sexual in nature. "It started in the business world, I think," my friend Cara said, "when women editors took male writers to lunch and paid, female stockbrokers took clients out, and so forth. Any explicit sexuality would taint the business relationship, so the friendship was destined to continue on a nonsexual plane. Since then I've noticed many such friendships in sports, among fellow professionals, and neighbors. My next-door neighbor is male, and we have coffee together occasionally; I water his plants when he goes on a business trip, and talk to him about his current girl friend — but we are just friends, that's all."

The trouble with male-female friendships is that the phenomenon is relatively new. Only a generation ago, women seldom had anything to do with men who weren't lovers or family. Now that this is changing, we don't quite know what the rules are anymore. Is it wise to turn a business friend into a lover? Does a sex episode spoil a friendship? Can a married man have a platonic friendship with a woman — and not be accused of infidelity? These and hundreds of other questions about this new experience almost beg for intuitive guidance.

FRIENDS VERSUS ACQUAINTANCES

Many of the people we know, even know well, are really only acquaintances, not friends. What determines the difference?

Depth. An acquaintance — whom you may see every day, indeed more often than you see your best friend — is limited to the superficial aspects of your existence either by circumstance or lack of interest in pursuing the relationship further. (An acquaintance may develop into a friend in time, but a friend cannot be turned back into an acquaintance; he becomes an ex-friend.) You may discuss weather, health, or the state of the Union with an acquaintance, but not fears that your marriage is shaky or that your job is on the line. An acquaintance may be a potential friend, but when your intuition tells you to leave well enough alone, give him only a minor role in your life.

EMPATHY

The experience of completely understanding and emotionally identifying with the feelings, motives, or thoughts of another person is almost totally an intuitive experience. To empathize with a person is to *intuit* how he or she feels.

Empathy is awareness that reaches beyond the conscious; it perceives what is not consciously perceived by the five senses: the hopes and disappointments of your friend. Often this awareness cannot be translated into words, but is reflected nevertheless in the actions you take and in your attitude.

Indeed, the essence of true friendship may lie in this capacity to empathize. Using your intuition will without doubt result in a greater ability to empathize and in a greater capacity for friendship. In fact, it will lead to a deeper compassion for all humankind.

CONSCIENCE

A leader is useless when he acts against the promptings of his own conscience.

— Mohandas K. Gandhi

I've included an examination of conscience in this chapter on friendship because there are no logical or intellectual guides to the proper way to act with a friend. Of course your conscience is called upon in many aspects of life, but I particularly want to highlight its importance when dealing with friends.

Conscience is the sense of right or wrong within. It is the awareness of moral goodness or fault concerning your conduct or attitudes. It is that small, insistent voice within you that you cannot shut out, that will not be silenced. No matter how brilliant the reasoning or logic you may use to defend the course of action you have taken, your conscience plugs away, pointing to the correct path, the path you should have taken even by your own standards.

When Shakespeare wrote "This above all, to thine own self be true," he probably knew that the intuitive, in the form of your conscience, will not let you rest if you are not true to your own self. Guilt, that old demon, plagues us mercilessly if we do not heed our conscience. Guilt is the *nagging* of our intuitive, the monkey on our back when we have acted against our principles with a friend, relative, or even a stranger.

People spend years in psychotherapy trying to overcome guilt. Free and open communication between your conscious and intuitive may be a quicker and more effective route for you.

When there is a wholesome dialogue between your two awareness systems, input from your nonverbal mind often nips in the bud those actions that are really against your moral grain and likely to result in guilt. A fringe benefit in developing your intuition may be a reasonably guilt-free life.

14

The Family
Experience

Family living magnifies and intensifies emotions such as love, anger, frustration, joy, hatred, sorrow, sympathy, envy, and jealousy — most of which cannot be dealt with rationally by adults and are even more perplexing for children. Intuition is an unbeatable tool in dealing with the vicissitudes of family life.

How can you fail to be impressed with the way animal mothers instinctively care for their young, how they seem to know exactly what is needed and when? In human beings, the nonverbal communication between the newborn and the mother is often miraculous. Some mothers understand what each cry of the infant means — can distinguish a hunger cry, a wet-diaper cry, a cry of pain — when to all others they sound exactly the same.

Long before the infant's brain has developed the power of thought or speech, the intuitive system is the bridge between the newborn and his environment. At the center is his mother, who is protector, nourisher, and teacher. For the child there is no competition between the conscious and the intuitive, no overshadowing by the left brain. Mother and child have a nonverbal communication system based on touch, sounds, and intuition. The infant whimpers and the mother understands: "He wants to go to sleep, he's tired." The mother leaves the room and the infant howls. He is saying, "Don't leave me, you are my main source of sustenance."

This mother/child rapport gradually diminishes as the child gets older and begins to talk and think. Is it because the left brain development preempts the intuitive signals? Or because the child is acquiring a more independent intuitive system of its own? We don't know. Still, the nonverbal communication between mother and child continues in some form long after infancy has passed. Perhaps it is never totally lost. Many mothers say that they can tell with one look what is troubling their child or teen-ager.

"Children are most intuitive because they haven't been programmed yet," a child psychologist once said to me. "They aren't ruined yet by adults, and don't look for what they are *supposed* to think."

Parents have special problems. They have their own insensitivities, fears, and dreams. Parents themselves are products of parents who were less than perfect. It's a wonder there are as many wholesome families as there are. When you think of all the ways your parents could have done better, you must realize how much better their parents could have been. You might also think of where you will fit on the scale of perfect parents. In trying to fulfill their own lives, parents sometimes forget the effect on their children.

One destructive course taken by parents is to consistently overshadow their children. For example, when the child is asked a question, the parent immediately answers. If the child starts to tell a story or incident, the parent takes over and finishes it. What does this do to the child's ego and confidence? It's telling the child nonverbally over and over, "You're an idiot. I'm afraid you'll say the wrong thing. I can't take any chances. I'll answer for you."

Another example: Often the parents' sheer talent and ability overpower their youngsters, who give up because they realize they can never emulate the wonderful father or mother. They withdraw, shrivel, and never fully flower. These parents, who desperately want their children to succeed, are bitter and frustrated. If your child isn't developing as beautifully as you expected, you might use your intuitive awareness to understand the problem and find a way to reach the turned-off child.

Sometimes the overshadowing is done by one of the brothers or sisters, and sibling rivalry takes over. The intuitive parent finds a way to sublimate competitive attitudes within the family that lead to hostility and even hatred. A working mother, an old friend, tells me that when she gets home her first act is to determine which of her kids needs the most loving — whose ego has been most battered and damaged, who needs her stroking and attention urgently. Then, after she has set things right, she goes about getting supper ready.

THE SENSITIVE PARENT

Some intuitive parents have a knack for responding to their children's problems. Florence and Zack, both educated, outgoing people, were the parents of a timid, self-effacing, overcautious son, Peter. With two younger girls in the family, there wasn't much time to think about or even discuss their son. Nevertheless, I had occasion to observe over the years how they intuitively handled the situation in tandem, each in his or her own way helping the boy to develop confidence.

Zack played touch football with Peter and taught him to wrestle, a skill he'd learned himself in college. Florence reported Peter's successes to the family with pride, and each bit of progress he made was counted as a success — but she did it in such a way that Peter was never aware he was getting special treatment.

Peter did develop confidence in time, but it wasn't until he was a freshman at Yale that I spoke to his parents about his transformation from a shy, unathletic boy to the top man on his high school's wrestling team and a boy so well-balanced that he was voted by his female classmates "Boy I'd Most Like to Be on a Deserted Island With." Neither Florence nor Zack was consciously aware that they had done anything special to help Peter. "Don't all parents do things to help their children become better adjusted?" was their attitude.

It is easier to be an intuitive parent than an insensitive one. Children start out without guile; much of what they feel is readily apparent if you look for it. The busy or well-meaning but rigid parent who only *listens* to what the child is saying but does not take into account what the child is telling him nonverbally will miss what the child really wants to communicate.

BEING INTUITIVE WITH YOUR SPOUSE

Open communication is desperately needed to make family life work. Yet there are so many things we don't say, so many emotions we can't express. It isn't "manly" to show weakness, so the husband doesn't show his vulnerability; indeed, he often creates an image of strength to fit the stereotype. His wife may adopt a role of deference, which is considered "womanly," but like her husband she too has deep emotional needs that do not fit the typical marital role.

Bill and Vera had a wonderful sex life in the early years of their marriage. Then the couple went to live with Vera's parents in a different town so that Vera might nurse her bedridden mother back to health. Bill took a new job in a law firm and was doing well. Vera enjoyed being with her mother and father again, and the older couple was very generous to them. Everything was going fine except that eight months after they moved in with Vera's parents, Bill became impotent; when they attempted to make love Bill would lose his erection almost immediately.

Vera struggled with the problem and then one day she had an intuitive flash. That evening she said to Bill: "We're moving out of this house. I'll get a nurse to take care of mother; we can afford it. We need to have our own house and our own life." That night they made love for the first time in six months.

Vera had correctly intuited that Bill's impotency had something to do with living with her parents. Bill had felt emasculated because her father was head of the house and he, Bill, was reduced to the role of another child.

Gladys, a housewife for twenty-one years, felt an emptiness in her marriage. Her husband, Matthew, was totally involved in his work and never discussed anything but household matters with her. Their two children were away at college.

Gladys spent many troubled hours strolling along the beach, looking for shells, thinking about her life. She was convinced her husband no longer loved her. Then one day, looking at a shell she knew what she must do.

Gladys went back to school. A few months after that she became a real-estate salesperson, one of the best in her area. She has again become the vital, bubbling woman that Matthew married, and her marriage has become stronger because she reached out into the world. She intuitively understood what was happening with her marriage — she had stopped being the interesting woman Matthew married — and her intuition also served her in finding a solution.

THE FAMILY CAN MAKE US OR BREAK US

The importance of the family at its best cannot be overestimated. It provides the support, education, development, security, and love that every human being needs. The family is a personal, intimate relationship, calling for give-and-take on every level. Open communication is desperately needed to make it work. Intuition can play a vital role.

You must have many examples of your own. Recall how at some crucial point in your life someone in your family came forward with just the right word or perfect action to help you. Perhaps it was some incident where you provided the help that made for family success or happiness. We don't always know on a conscious level what we need and so we are often surprised by our strong emotional reaction to a small kindness.

In the give-and-take of family life, it is not only the parents who must be intuitive; the sooner children recognize that parents have needs and weaknesses too, the better and stronger the family!

The family is not a static or rigid organization. It's constantly changing: New members are added by birth or marriage, and voids created by death, divorce, or alienation. There are power shifts and power struggles, old alliances and voting blocs. The family may look serene from the outside, but it's a caldron of wants and needs on the inside that constantly call for all the grace and kindness we can muster.

The help that intuitive sensitivity can provide can make all the difference. A family functioning at its best is an inspiration for all humanity.

DEATH AND BEYOND

In his book *Living Your Dying*, Stanley Keleman points out that we are always dying a bit, always giving things up or having them taken away. His thesis is, in brief, that we should not block off the intuitive awareness we all have about dying. We know we are going to die eventually, but we avoid the subject so that the conscious will not be confronted by it.

Your intuitive sense knows all about dying and it can help you accept gracefully the inevitability of death. When you accept this awareness, you are able to experience a fuller life. As you absorb the finiteness of your life, each day increases in value.

Here is an old Yiddish expression so often uttered to the bereaved at funerals: "You shouldn't know from this kind of trouble again." It is so touching and sincere, yet if you follow the logic, since we're all going to die, you would have to die before any of the others to avoid the experience.

Recently I attended the wake for an old friend. Seated weeping on one side of the casket was his young daughter, a college junior, distraught with her grief. What to say? What can anyone say?

I just shook her hand — and then, much to the surprise of everyone around us, she smiled softly and embraced me, and said, "Oh thank you so much for remembering."

I had intuitively done something that I hadn't consciously planned, and as a matter of fact I surprised myself: I had given her the secret "Fun Club" handshake. When she and my daughter were little girls, her father and I were enthusiastic founders of a "secret" organization dedicated to having fun. What great memories of her father were brought back with that handshake. How invaluable the intuitive!

15

Personal Style

Who can forget the image of poet Marianne Moore in black cape and tricorne hat cheering in the bleachers at Yankee Stadium? Or Eleanor Roosevelt, whose personal style was practical, intellectual, homey, lending assurance to millions of women comforted by her very stodginess? Or Bianca Jagger, in a sequined tuxedo, photographed dancing at Studio 54, or Bella Abzug's signature hat, in an era that eschews large hats, which permits her to stand out in a crowd.

Your personal style tells a great deal about you, sometimes more than you care to divulge. How you dress, where you live, how your home is furnished, what your car looks like, your manner of speaking, the way you comb your hair — all reflect not only what you think of yourself, but how closely you conform to society's expectations, the state of your exchequer, what part of the country you live in, what you do for a living, and whether or not you care what other people think of you.

We are, for the most part, hemmed in by countless rules and regulations calculated to make us all conform. Nevertheless, the eternal desire of man to establish his individuality seems to burst forth. Even the corporate executive so conscious of his image will occasionally wear a colorful tie, hang modern paintings on his office walls, or, in the privacy of his home, indulge in black silk pajamas.

A recent publishing phenomenon has been the proliferation of books that purport to tell you how to "dress for success." Dress this way, they tell you, and you will wow the executive board. Dress another way and you are doomed to remain in the mailroom or secretarial pool.

Should you consider this in putting yourself together, in evolving a personal style that is harmonious with your inner self?

The answer is not easy. To some extent we must all pare down (or beef up) our personal style to fit our life situation. This is where your intuition can be of assistance to you; if it rejects the style imposed upon you by the requirements of your job, take heed, for a far deeper challenge may be revealed to you.

Indeed, if your present career or living arrangement is imposing uncomfortable constrictions upon your personal style, it may be time to reconsider your life goals. If you are masking the real you, trying to cover up your real preferences, for whatever reason, the effort may make demands that are costly — that may even lead to medical problems.

CRAIG'S STORY

The novice in the business world often does not realize the relevance of appearance, or that one must sometimes subdue the individual in ourselves for the good of the team. Craig, a young man just out of college and hired by a multi-national corporation as a management trainee, appeared the first day on his job with a trim beard, although he had been hired clean-shaven. The personnel director casually mentioned that company rules did not permit trainees or management to sport beards. When he went home that evening, Craig was fuming. He told his parents the company rules were an infringement upon his freedom of self-expression. He talked about going to court to challenge the company's right to dictate how he looked.

"Look," his father said, "it's their ball game. If you don't like the rules, you can drop out of the game."

"Shave off your beard, stay in the company, and gradually, as you work your way up in the hierarchy, you will acquire power to change the rules. Who knows, ten years from now, maybe all executives will be *required* to grow beards," his mother pitched in.

"If you make a fuss about this, you will draw adverse attention to yourself too early in the game," advised his uncle. "Feel your way around and learn the ropes. Everybody makes mistakes when they are new on the job, and if you have already drawn unpleasant attention to yourself, these mistakes can be enough to ruin your chances."

Despite his youth, Craig was in good touch with himself and "slept on it," as he later told me. Two weeks later he left the company and went back to graduate school with the intention of staying in academia and becoming a professor. "It just came to me that the beard was just a small part of my personal style that would have been challenged in some way by the company," he told me. His intuitive mind made it clear that he was not willing to make the adjustments necessary to fit into Amalgamated Widgets; that he would be more comfortable in a profession where a bit of eccentricity was accepted.

ROSALIND'S ATTITUDE

Rosalind G., however, could hardly wait to join the United States Army after high school. Both her brother and one sister had enlisted in the army, and her sister had been sent to a base in Europe, which seemed an exciting prospect to Rosalind. She not only welcomed the security of regular hours, regular meals, well-defined rules, but she was also proud to wear the uniform. Conforming to the rules was not an infringement of her personal style. She saw rules as necessary for the functioning of the whole. Her personal style, she felt, was within, and her co-workers knew and appreciated that in her; she saw no need to display her individuality upon her person.

And so we have two diametrically opposed attitudes, yet each right for that person. They were each intuitively able to make the adjustments necessary for securing the appropriate life-style.

Determine your personal style early in your career and stick to it, adapting any new twists in fashion to your basic style. There is no way to do this except intuitively. No logic in the world can tell you that you are a tweedy person or an ethnic type or that you will feel better in conservative business suits. You just have to close your eyes and grope for what feels right for you.

Your personal style is based on an image or images you have of yourself, including a future image. Try to picture the kind of image you want for yourself, both present and future. You may be a secretary now but aiming to become an account executive. You have the problem of presenting yourself now as a competent secretary with the potential of rising higher. That means you may not allow yourself the luxury of wearing jeans or a backless sundress to the office even if they are permitted. That may be OK for the secretary, but *out* for someone who is hoping the boss will visualize her making a presentation before a client.

In the business world you can't totally ignore fashion trends. To ignore certain fashion dictates marks you as totally "out of it," behind the times, fixed in another period. To a certain extent, you must comply. You should not, for example, wear a miniskirt when they have been out of fashion for years. It marks you as hopelessly passé and a bit gauche. Remember the sack dress? False eyelashes? Platform shoes? Stiletto heels? Throw them all out (or donate them to a thrift shop) or risk being considered behind the times mentally as well.

Men's clothes have more fashion longevity, which is an advantage. Men's daytime styles are almost classic and therefore trend-proof. The only changes are likely to be tie width or lapel size. Leisure clothes are more apt to date men, so donate your plaid trousers and "leisure suits" to a local charity. If your company is the kind where a lot of business is done on the golf course or at the hunting lodge, keep attuned to what top management is wearing. Funny how the smallest gaffe can mark you as an outsider. Once you know what the customs are, however, you can take liberties with them. This too is intuitive — you get a feeling about how much you personally can get away with in modifying the acceptable attire.

THE WHITE PANACHE

Make sure your deviations from current fashion are done with panache. Originally, *panache* meant a cluster of feathers or a plume worn on the helmets of knights. In the Middle Ages, during a great battle in France, one side was losing badly, the soldiers were demoralized, and a partial retreat was about to turn into a rout, when their captain, who wore a white plume in his helmet, rode among the soldiers on horseback, sword in hand, shouting, "Follow the white panache!" He wheeled his horse around and drove back into the thick of battle. His men, inspired, followed, and fought on to victory.

Since then, the term *panache* has meant a kind of cocky verve, a self-confident leadership. The white panache that rode into battle represented to the soldiers the kind of self-assured bravery, the idea that how we fight the battle is as important as whether we win or lose. Significantly, in the legend, the white panache did indeed help win the day, for the soldiers would not have fought on without this kind of leadership. One marvels at the intuitive flash that led the captain of the white panache to this act of bravery that so inspired his soldiers.

If your exterior style is in harmony with your inner or real style, you will have fewer conflicts and unexplained anxieties. It is only when we are forced to entertain a style that is not part of our nature that we run into trouble.

How do you determine what is indeed your "true" nature? A clue that you are not coming across to others in accordance with your inner nature may surface when you're a bit drunk and people tell you how different you seem. Another is the content of your dreams, which may disclose a more adventurous nature or a more pacifist one than you allow yourself in waking life. A third and most basic one is, are you really happy with yourself? But remember, the search for our true selves goes on forever and is part of the adventure of life.

16

Things to Think About

Intuition affects many aspects of your life in addition to those covered in the previous chapters. It can help you in virtually everything you do.

SPORTS AND THE INNER YOU

In 1974, Tim Gallwey authored a book called *The Inner Game of Tennis* and startled the world of sports by suggesting a new approach to playing tennis better. Too much intellectual effort to control the body is self-defeating. It is better, the author said, to develop an awareness of the body and pay attention to its feedback. In his own way, Gallwey was talking about the use of the intuitive system in sports, and the things he wrote about have had great impact on methods of teaching tennis today.

There is great need for the use of intuition in sports. As we learned in chapter six, "Biofeedback Breakthrough," internal processes — the heartbeat, peristalsis, digestion, secretion of enzymes, to mention but a few — function quite well without any conscious direction. In fact, when there *is* conscious involvement or concern, the functions are usually negatively affected: Worry can upset the digestive system, fear will accelerate the heartbeat, and anxiety can raise blood pressure.

What has this got to do with sports? The ability to perform a complicated athletic feat lies in the coordination of body and the mind. Alas, for many of us there is too much *head* in our game. We do not give our bodies a chance to take over and perform.

By giving our bodies a chance, we allow the intuitive system to have greater influence. No matter what your sport is, there is evidence enough on hand to indicate that you can improve by letting intuition play a greater part. For years this phenomenon was referred to by physical education specialists as the "kinesthetic sense" — the knowledge inherent in the muscles themselves. Using intuition means that, for example, in learning a golf swing you let your body take over and do not try to memorize the step-by-step instructions of just how your body should be poised in each phase of the swing. Or, in a swan dive you would trust the body to sense the exact moment to arch your back and spread your arms.

Many knowledgeable coaches today (notice they are called coaches, not teachers, perhaps a significant semantic difference that implies that teaching sports is not inherently a logical, pedantic function) believe that you can improve performance if you inhibit thought direction and allow your intuitive system to help you by applying what it knows.

Watch great athletes in action. Specifically, watch a fine pro performing in the sport in which you wish to excel. Do not *think* about it, just watch and absorb. Later, visualize the performance over again in your mind. Then visualize *yourself* performing the same activity the same way.

Afterward, when you are out on the court, field, or

diamond, don't think about it; just let your body and intuition take over. Your right brain has assimilated the essentials of your hero's performance, and in time, all other factors being equal, this knowledge will be translated into your own performance. (Of course, you'll never shoot baskets like "Dr. J." if you aren't seven feet tall, but don't let that deter you. You can still shoot the best baskets a five-foot-seven person ever shot.)

Sportscaster Mel Allen once told me that the most spectacular sporting feats he had ever witnessed *had* to be intuitive, because there was never enough time for the athlete to think it all out.

And Dr. Barbara Kolonay, a psychologist who works mainly with athletes, told the *New York Times* that she recently taught relaxation techniques to a gym class in New Orleans before they played basketball, improving the foul shooting from sixty-eight to seventy-four percent in one week. There is no doubt in my mind that the relaxation increased intuitive input with the results indicated.

LOVE AND MARRIAGE

Love and marriage pose some of the most important decisions in your life. Many readers may be skeptical, conceding that though marriage may indeed involve a decision, love "just happens." But, actually, *you love the one you choose to love,* even though you may not be aware that you have made a choice. Physical attraction may create instantaneous infatuation, but it does not create love. Love is a much slower and more deliberate process.

Love starts with the need, usually unconscious, to find someone to share things with on the most basic and intimate level, someone with whom to share your life and dreams, someone who has the same need and is searching for someone like you.

Note "someone like you," not you. At the risk of outraging

countless romantics, don't believe there is a "one and only" you must find. There are thousands of people out there who can become your one and only, that is, thousands who possess the qualities and the needs that enable any one of them to become a suitable life partner for you.

As you develop more and more shared experience with your loved one, you do in time become unique to each other and then — and only then — the "one and only."

This all happens, of course, on an unconscious level. The participants in the love experience are usually so involved with the magic of it that they are oblivious of everything but the experience itself.

LET YOUR INTUITION DO THE CHOOSING

The selection of a lover and the monitoring of the development of love is almost exclusively intuitive, which may be why so much conflict, turmoil, and emotion are often involved. Sometimes the love and courtship experience entails a struggle between the left and the right brain systems. The ideal mate chosen by reason and logic may be rejected by your intuition — or vice versa.

When there is a conflict between what reason dictates and where your feelings lie, always let your intuition do the choosing. Intuition perceives the whole picture. It sees relevance and consequences that the conscious misses. Your intuition knows all about you and your needs. It remains unimpressed with the trappings of success or appearance, no matter what reason may be urging you to do.

INTUITIVE MARRIAGE

Marriage is the open, public pronouncement of your choice, an acknowledgment to the world that there is love and that you are prepared to make a formal commitment to each other. This is very different from the private commitment many young people today believe in, because it involves a dimension of responsibility and obligation, which has been, since time immemorial, the basic reason for marriage.

Marriage calls for the utmost in cooperation and sensitivity. When one's happiness and life-style are interlocked with those of another, and you are both aiming for that special kind of friendship called love, intuitive sensitivity must be brought into play more than in any other facet of your life.

"LOOK BEFORE YOU LEAP"

If you are thinking seriously of sharing your life with a certain person, this exercise can be useful in helping you reach your decision; it helps you "look before you leap."

1. Perform the Basic Warm-up in a place where you will not be disturbed. Then, using the technique of visualization (see chapter eleven, "You Can Stay Healthy"), play out an inner movie of what your life would be like with that person. Lights (off), camera, action!

2. Put yourself in the "starring role" of husband or wife and play out a full day with your prospective spouse: Visualize yourself having breakfast, working, loving, quarreling, watching television, and going to bed together.

3. Change the scenery and play your part among his or her friends, relatives, and colleagues. Switch and visualize him or her alongside you with *your* friends, relatives, and colleagues. Does he or she fit in easily? Do the others accept your loved one?

4. Visualize the children you may have together. How you will bring them up together. How you will educate and care for them.

5. Picture the two of you in old age, in sickness, in tragedy. Do you give emotional sustenance to each other?

The more detail you can put into this mental script, the better your intuitive feedback will be. If you find you have not received a clear feeling about your intended and how your future shapes up together, repeat the exercise.

ADVANCED TECHNIQUES

The techniques described below will probably not be used by you. Nevertheless, it may be useful for you to know about them because they are in many ways extensions of methods already explained. If you yearn for a higher level of awareness, you may want to investigate them further.

De-automatization. In this technique, you train yourself to look at an object as though you were seeing it for the first time. This is a method often used by mystics and spiritual leaders to break away from the domination of the rational conditioned mind in sensing the world around them. In order to seek a deeper reality, the disciple strives to break away from the automatic, conditioned reaction that has been learned by the conscious mind.

In a highly civilized society we learn to see many things in a generalized way. We do not have the time to investigate and appreciate the properties of a chair, for example. We do not see the wood grain in the chair, nor do we notice how many rungs it has — or if it has any — or the beauty of its workmanship. You have undoubtedly sat on many different chairs in the course of your day. Do you remember what they looked like? Do you remember anything about them at all? Probably not. We perceive and experience only the essential: that it is for sitting upon. We deal in symbols, in terms of usefulness, and so we miss a great deal of the "thingness" of the object.

In de-automatization, the process is reversed. A chair would be contemplated for a long period of time, hours or even days. Perceptions are intensified. Automatic, shallow, casual observation is discouraged. The fullness of detail, color, texture, flavor is discovered.

This technique brings a sense of newness to life. Everything seems fresh and new, and there may be a feeling of rebirth into a different and new world, a great sense of exhilaration and wonder. The mystics compare this to childhood; when a child perceives even ordinary things for the first time he is mystified and full of wonder.

Renunciation. This is a technique that unburdens us of the material world. It is the acceptance of isolation, silence, poverty, and chastity, and it can be a powerful tool to use to achieve de-automatization. By eliminating attention to material stimuli and the minutiae of daily living, renunication heightens the potential for religious experience. In fact, it has been adopted by religious orders through the ages in order to focus upon the purity of God and the eternal. It is also a very dramatic way to blot out left brain activity. Needless to say, I do not recommend this for the ordinary everyday variety of intuition-seeker.

Brainstorming. This technique, which has been discussed in an earlier chapter, can be put to good use by the individual as well as the group. It is a lively technique for stimulating creative ideas and is based on the free and easy production of such without judgment on them. Widely used in industry, schools, think tanks, and advertising, brainstorming has been very successful in the production of new concepts and new products.

This same technique can be used by you in solitude. The essential key to the technique is the suppression of the left brain judge. Brainstorming is not only for problem solving, but also stimulates intuitive participation and brings it to center stage.

INTUITIVE CONSCIOUSNESS-RAISING GROUP

An effective and fun way to improve your intuitive awarenes is to form an Intuitive Consciousness-Raising Group. When other people who share your interest are willing to do the recommended exercises along with you, you increase the potential for better results. The exchange of ideas is beneficial and the exercises may take on new meaning and excitement when shared with others. If you wish to form such a group, here are some simple rules to guide you:

1. Plan for no more than ten sessions. You will find that having a definitive period of time to cover the work and reach the goals appeals to the participants and encourages seriousness.

2. Give each person five or ten minutes to talk about his or her problem, without interruptions. Highlight how they feel when they talk about the problem and/or when they grapple with it. Avoid being judgmental and stick to the topic at hand.

3. At the end of the presentation, the host or group leader picks up, searching out the lesson to be gained from each person's intuitive feedback.

4. The exercises in this book may be performed before or after discussion. In one of the groups I was told about, the exercises were performed first, as sort of a warm-up. It was highly effective in relaxing the group members for the discussion period.

5. This book may be used as a guide, but any topic that interests the participants may serve as the take-off for the session.

In the group I mentioned above, one session each was devoted to the use of intuition in health, problem solving, careers, family and marriage, and dreams; the final session was devoted to a demonstration of biofeedback by a local university specialist. There is no reason, however, why another group might not care to devote a session to business problems, sex, children, mid-life crises, career changes or whatever is upper-most on the minds of the group. Intuition is an infinitely flexible tool and related to every life problem.

Intuitive consciousness-raising groups can be formed anywhere. It is no more necessary to be a professional teacher or analyst in order to form one than it was necessary for a professional to lead a women's liberation consciousness-raising group so common in the seventies. The goals are similar: the sharing of special experience and knowledge where there are no formal textbooks, classes, or college problems. This has changed somewhat for the women's movement: Many colleges and universities now have formal Women's Studies programs, and a few even offer a bachelor's or master's program. Perhaps, in time, intuitive knowledge will be accorded similar im-portance. In the meantime, you can spread the word about this unrecognized and unrespected method of acquiring and using knowledge.

HUMANITY AND INTUITION

Your intuitive system controls those qualities that make you a human being: courage, altruism, compassion, benevo-lence, sensitivity, kindness, love, companionship, empathy, sympathy, remorse, grief, joy, anger, scorn, hatred, nostalgia, yearning, and ambition.

None of the above come from thinking. They all have their roots deep in our nonverbal being and grow from an awareness outside of conscious direction. All of the emotions that give your life shape and meaning, color and flair well up from a triggering apparatus that you do not control consciously.

Feeling is the living experience! Imagine a life without emotion. You would be a machine, inanimate, apathetic, and numb. Yet we spend so little time wondering where feeling comes from or what it means.

To reach your full potential you must develop and build the bridge between your two systems of awareness and then use it to achieve the success and happiness you so richly deserve.

Suggested
Reading

Abel, A.M. *Talks with the Great Composers*. Garmisch – Partenkirchen, Germany: G.E. Schroeder – Verlag, 1964.

Anderson, B.F. *Cognitive Psychology*. New York: Academic Press, 1975.

Arieti, S. *Creativity: The Magic Synthesis*. New York: Basic Books, 1976.

Barron, F. *Creative Person and Creative Process*. New York: Holt, Rinehart, and Winston, 1969.

Bensen, Herbert. *The Relaxation Response*. New York: William Morrow & Co., 1975.

Berger, John. *Ways of Seeing*. New York: Penguin Books, 1972.

Bettleheim, Bruno. *The Uses of Enchantment*. New York: Vintage Books, 1977.

Brown, Barbara. *Supermind*. New York: Harper & Row, 1980.

———. *New Mind, New Body*. New York: Harper & Row, 1974.

Buzan, Tony. *Use Both Sides of Your Brain*. New York: E. P. Dutton, 1976.

Castaneda, Carlos. *The Teachings of Don Juan*. University of California Press, 1968.

Coddington, Mary. *In Search of the Healing Energy*. New York: Warner Destiny, 1978.

Corriere, R. and Hart, J. *The Dream Makers*. New York: Funk & Wagnalls, 1977.

deBono, E. *Lateral Thinking*. New York: Harper & Row, 1970.

Faraday, Ann. *The Dream Game*. New York: Penguin Books, 1974.

Fast, Julius. *Body Language*. New York: M. Evans and Company, 1970.

Gallwey, Tim. *The Inner Game of Tennis*. New York: Random House, 1974.

Ghiselin, B., ed. *The Creative Process*. Berkeley: University of California Press, 1952.

Gowen, J.C. *Development of the Creative Individual*. San Diego: R. Knapp, 1972.

Green, Elmer and Alyce. *Beyond Biofeedback*. New York: Delacorte Press, 1977.

Hoopes, Ann and Townsend. *Eye Power*. New York: Alfred A. Knopf, 1979.

Jaynes, J. *The Origin of Consciousness in the Breakdown of the Bicameral Mind*. Boston: Houghton Mifflin, 1976.

Journal of Creative Behavior. Buffalo, N.Y.: The Creative Education Foundation, Inc. Vol. I, 1967 to date.

Jung, C.G. *Memories, Dreams, Reflections*. New York: Vintage, 1961.

Jung, C.G. *The Portable Jung*. New York: Viking, 1971.

Keleman, Stanley. *Living Your Dying*. New York: Random House, 1976.

Khatena, J. *The Creatively Gifted Child*. New York: Vantage Press, 1977.

Kneller, G. *The Art and Science of Creativity*. New York: Holt, Rinehart, and Winston, 1965.

Koestler, A. *The Act of Creation*. New York: Macmillan, 1964.

Krippern, Stanley. *The Song of the Siren*. New York: Harper & Row, 1975.

Luce, Gay Gaer. *Body Time*. New York: Pantheon Books, 1971.

McLeester, Dick. *Welcome to the Magic Theater*. Amherst, Mass.: Food for Thought Publications, 1975.

Maslow, A. *Towards a Psychology of Being*. New York: Van Nostrand, 1968.

May, Rollo. *The Courage to Create*. New York: Norton, 1975.

Ornstein, Robert. *The Mind Field*. New York: Grossman Publishers, 1976.

———. *The Psychology of Consciousness*. San Francisco: W. H. Freeman, 1972.

Osborn, A.F. *Applied Imagination*. New York: Scribners, 1953.

Parnes, S. *Creative Behavior Guidebook*. New York: Scribners, 1967.

Pfeiffer, Carl. *Zinc and Other Micro Nutrients*. New Canaan, Conn.: Keats Publishing Co., 1978.

Reik, Theodor. *Listening with the Third Ear*. New York: Farrar, Strauss, 1948.

Rogers, C. *On Becoming a Person*. Boston: Houghton Mifflin, 1961.

Russell, Peter. *The Brain Book*. New York: Hawthorn Books, Inc., 1979.

Sagan, Carl. *The Dragons of Eden*. New York: Random House, 1977.

Samuels, M. and Samuels, N. *Seeing with the Mind's Eye*. New York: Random House, 1975.

Taylor, Gordon Rattray. *Natural History of the Mind*. New York: Dutton, 1979.

Thomas, Lewis. *The Medusa and The Snail*. New York: Viking, 1979.

Toffler, A., ed. *Learning for Tomorrow*. New York: Random House, 1974.

Torrance, E.P. and Myers, R.E. *Creative Learning and Teaching*. New York: Dodd Mead, 1970.

Virshup, Evelyn. *Right Brain People in a Left Brain World*. Los Angeles: Guild of Tutors Press, 1978.

Wallas, G. *The Art of Thought*. New York: Harcourt Brace, 1926.